PERSIST

Yes! Persist!

PERSIST

In Praise of the Creative Spirit in a World Gone Mad with Commerce

Peter Clothier

Parami Press, LLC
Vancouver, Washington, USA

Published by
Parami Press, LLC
PO Box 65372
Vancouver, Washington 98665

ISBN: 978-0-9779774-1-3
LCCN: 2009936102

Front cover by Jeff Koegel, Laguna Beach, Calif.

Printed in the United States of America

To all my teachers and to those who, like myself, seek to use their creative talent to make this world a better place, in ways both great and small.

Contents

ACKNOWLEDGMENTS

There is surely nothing more delightfully refreshing—to both giver and receiver—than a heartfelt expression of gratitude. I consider myself fortunate indeed to have so much to be thankful for and so many people to thank for their love and for the wisdom they have shared with me.

A good place for me to start giving thanks is with three wonderful groups of people I have come to think of as my surrogate *sanghas* (there's more about this lovely concept later in the book). Suffice it to say at this point that—while I understand that it has come to be used too loosely in the West—I hope to cause no offense if I borrow this term from the Buddhist teachings to add some special quality to my description of these loving and mutually supportive communities of like-minded individuals.

The first of them is a community of men called The ManKind Project in which I learned how the shadow side of my psyche works—sometimes in less than useful ways—and learned a great deal more about what it means to be a man in the world today. The members of The ManKind Project now number in the tens of thousands worldwide, but my gratitude goes particularly to those many with whom I have worked intimately, sometimes painfully, towards self-knowledge, and to those I have been privileged to help work toward their own. They have all been my teachers.

The second is Artists Matters, the group of artists with whom my wife, Ellie Blankfort, and I have been working for more than a dozen years, meeting monthly in our home to share, generously and often fearlessly, the joys and tribulations of our creative lives. Much of what I have learned from them is reflected in this book.

And the third, the Laguna Sangha, is more in the tradition of a true *sangha*. It is the meditation and study group that meets each Sunday near my home in Laguna Beach, California, to sit for an hour and talk for another hour not only about the teachings of the Buddha but also about other important things in life. From these good friends I have learned much about discipline, showing up, dedication, and, not least, compassion.

I am particularly grateful to our *sangha's* teacher, Thanissaro Bhikkhu, Abbott of the Metta Forest Monastery in Valley Center, California, who comes once a month to sit in our circle and instruct us. A man of enormous generosity and compassion—and an extraordinarily fine, prolific writer himself—he has shared with us more profound wisdom over the years than I could ever possibly absorb. I trust that some small part of it is reflected in these essays.

I am grateful to my readers, especially those who follow my blog, "The Buddha Diaries" (TheBuddhaDiaries.com), who are generous and thoughtful in their comments. I value this circle of friends whom I have never met but whose presence I deeply appreciate as a true gift.

I am grateful to my daughter, Sarah, for having been one of my most valued and beloved teachers; and to my wife, Ellie, for the love she never fails to show me, for her devotion to the cause of art and artists, and for the wide knowledge and understanding that she brings to her avocation as a mentor to creative people of all kinds, not excluding myself.

I would be remiss not to express my gratitude to Bill Lasarow, publisher, editor, and friend, at whose instigation a number of these essays were first written and published in their original form in his magazine, *Artscene*. And finally, I am grateful to Paul Gerhards of Parami Press, whose enthusiasm and support have shaped the preparation of this book, and to the team he assembled to put it all together. May all these good people find the path to true happiness in their lives.

INTRODUCTION

Where We Begin

This is a book about the creative life. It's written with love, appreciation, compassion, and respect for those who dedicate themselves to the creative work they do. In good part, it's a book about what it takes for me, a writer, to keep doing what I do—with passion, with love, with a sense of its importance—in a world that seems on the one hand to encourage the creative spirit and on the other to reward its outcomes too often with indifference and neglect. I need to keep writing just as others need to keep making art, singing, dancing, making music . . . and this book is about what it takes, in such a world, for the artist to persist. (I'll be using the word artist a lot, by the way. I intend it to embrace not only visual artists who make paintings, sculptures, photographs, prints, and so on, but also writers like myself, musicians, actors, dancers . . . all those who consider the creative process to be central to their lives and an important part of who they are.)

Through years of experience as a writer, teacher, art school dean, and sympathetic observer of the lives of my fellow artists, I have come to recognize that the huge majority of us will experience some measure of discouragement and rejection. We are nourished on dreams of success that most frequently prove to be a fantasy. That's simply the way things are. So we learn to take care of ourselves, knowing that nobody else is going to do it for us and that we are fortunate to have a calling that can contribute to the happiness of others in today's often unkind world.

Though I have had this little book of essays in mind for quite some time, I have to confess that I have never been sure what it was actually about until now. I have always loved writing in this form, but I realized that a collection of essays would not be much of a book in and of itself. A book needs focus—a purpose of its own—and, while I recognized a special attachment to these pieces of writing that now span more than thirty years, and while I felt in my bones that they shared a common theme, I have been pretty much content to sit around, waiting for them to tell me what they wanted to be.

Then it came to me one evening recently when I was sitting together with my wife and the group of a dozen or so artists who come to our home every month for discussion and mutual support: these pieces of writing are all in one way or another about survival—the survival of the creative spirit in a world that rewards only a very lucky few. It's a particularly rough moment in history for the lesser-known artist and the lesser-known writer. The national economy is in crisis, and, like other small businesses, the art business is suffering. Art dealers are not scrambling over the latest hot young artist to come out of graduate school as they once did. Publishers seem interested only in the already successful writer or those writers who bring with them a name that is guaranteed to attract the interest of the book-buying public. Artists who were once able to scrape together a living with a combination of modest sales and part- or full-time jobs now find it harder to survive. The work of musicians can easily be pirated and made instantly available to anyone who owns a cell phone, and so on and so forth.

Consider a handful of the stories that I heard at our group meeting, and see if they don't sound distressingly familiar: one of our number had planned to retire, finally, that month and to devote her full attention to her studio work. She had planned to say goodbye to a job she had never much liked but that paid the bills; then, like so many others, she had watched her financial retirement plan wither, and she could not afford to leave. Another of our group had just been laid off from her teaching job; her husband, in his search for employment, had needed to accept a job a thousand miles away. A third had also seen her husband lose his job and was devoting much of what would have been her own studio time and energy to support him in his search for a new direction. Tough times, indeed—and not only for artists.

Remarkably, though, I heard no note of self-pity. What I heard was more like courage, perseverance, and dedication. The need to be involved in the creative act was predominant in the lives of each artist in our small group, if only because—in a phrase I often return to—that is what they are given to do. They will not abandon that dedication, no matter what. Without the creative act, these artists' lives would simply not make sense.

What happens to dedicated, workaday artists in a world that so often neglects their talents even as it richly rewards a handful of sometimes undeserving superstars? It's this phenomenon that I have been writing about. How is the creative spirit to survive in an art world that has had, over the past half-century, increasingly less to do with art and artists than with money, celebrity, and marketing?

I'm sad to say that I lost the first piece I wrote on this topic: it clearly belonged in this collection. It was called "A Word for the Amateur" and was published more than thirty years ago in one of those small, ephemeral magazines that were the life-blood of much underground art writing before the Internet came along. It was seized on with enthusiasm soon after its publication by an organization of women artists and reprinted in their newsletter.

The essay provoked some interesting controversy in the 1970s. At that time, I was not only an observer of the art scene in Los Angeles but also the dean of what was then Otis Art Institute

of Los Angeles County (now Otis College of Art and Design). I
heard a lot about the need for students to be "professional" and
understood that this was well intended: they should take themselves seriously as artists and present themselves seriously to
the world. But this was a time when art schools and university
art departments were beginning to disgorge thousands of artists each year, all of whom now aimed to be "professional." The
schools were providing them with expensive degrees to prove
their credentials and letting them loose in an art market that
had room for only a tiny minority of them. You'd have to be will-
fully blind to ignore the fact that at most ten of every hundred
students stood a chance in hell of actually becoming *professional*
in the commonly accepted sense of the word: earning a living
through their practice. The other 90 percent would need to deal
with the frustration of the expectations they had been fed. The
whole thing began to seem disingenuous and wrong. So I wrote
"A Word for the Amateur."

By the late twentieth century, of course, the word *amateur*
had acquired a bad reputation in the art world. To be an amateur
meant to be a Sunday painter, a third-rate artist whose work was
beyond the pale of acceptability in the mainstream. The amateur
was one possessed of neither the skills nor the seriousness of purpose of the so-called professional—who was supposedly clued in
to the arcane secrets of the contemporary art scene.

I wanted to revive something of the original meaning of a word
I considered to have a certain historical nobility. Most eminent
scientists of earlier centuries, as well as a good number of artists
and writers, had been amateurs—lovers, really—in the original,
etymological sense. These were people dedicated with passionate
altruism to the life of the mind or to their art with no thought or
prospect of financial reward. Professions, I argued in my essay, are
for lawyers and doctors and the like—people who can realistically
expect to earn a living by the fruits of their expertise.

I was happy to find my opinion echoed recently by the artist

Dan Graham, now widely honored by the critics and exhibited internationally. "[Graham] dislikes," read an article by Randy Kennedy in the *New York Sunday Times* (June 25, 2009), "being called a conceptual artist, and says *he is not a professional in any sense, calling his art his 'passionate hobby.'*" Precisely. (The italics are mine.)

Earning a living with art is a fanciful expectation for the vast majority of those we certify as artists with the award of a college degree, thanks largely to a self-supporting, self-perpetuating system that provides teaching jobs for otherwise unemployable artists. What results is a disconnect between what students have been led to expect and the realties that await them . . . and there is an army of the walking wounded out there to prove this point. Our culture celebrates creativity from the earliest age in schools. Children are encouraged to express themselves even before they learn the ABC's that enable them to do it. So many of our brightest young people dream of careers in music, acting, film, and television, but later find themselves in a career market that offers scant possibility of fulfilling the dream they have been fraudulently urged to dream. I live in Hollywood and go to restaurants. I talk to the servers.

This collection of essays is intended to celebrate and encourage these amateurs—or rather, more honestly, us. Because, though I myself have been fortunate enough to enjoy a good measure of success as a writer, I too am confronted with the reality of a publishing world in which many thousands of worthy writers flounder against the formidable rocks of commercial demands. If I write about the survival of the creative spirit in such a cultural context, it's because I myself have needed to develop strategies and mind-sets that enable me to persevere with a sense of dedication, self-respect, and persistence that might otherwise seem foolishly quixotic. These essays have been written to remind myself, at moments of discouragement, that I am, first, foremost, and always, a writer—if only because that is what I have been given to do.

THE BIG LIE

Written after "Write For Your Life," a workshop at the Holiday Inn in Hollywood, California, in 1986.

Let me acknowledge first an enormous debt of gratitude to Lawrence Block. Many, I trust, will know Larry as the extraordinarily skilled, prolific, and deservedly popular author of dozens of mystery novels and thrillers and, for many years, a contributor to *Writer's Digest* magazine. I know him also as the man who introduced me to a whole new way of thinking about myself as a writer. He opened the door for life without the day job in academia that had consumed the better part of my time and energies until I was well into middle age despite the fact that I had known, since the age of twelve, that I was supposed to be a writer. Like the vast majority of creative people, I suspect, I had put aside my passion in favor of what I saw to be the practical necessity of earning a living to support a home and family.

Here's the story: I had just lost my job, the third in a multi-year succession of academic positions of increasing status and responsibility. I had been, to be utterly honest, pretty much kicked out, as I had been from my two previous jobs. I had refused to conform to academic standards and expectations. I had published *poetry*, for God's sake, rather than scholarly articles. As a dean, I had continually provoked the wrath of vice presidents with my demands for adequate funding for my faculty and programs. I had alienated boards with my stubborn refusal to go along with what I considered to be their ill-advised policies. Eased out of these jobs, I managed to put a conveniently plausible construction on the facts each time in order to rescue my own sense of self-respect, but in retrospect I recognize that I was simply closing my ears to what the experiences were trying to tell me: you do not belong in academia; you were never meant to be here in the first place, and it's time to take the risk you always lacked the fortitude to take—to be a writer. It was Larry Block who helped me hear that message.

At the time—this was in the mid-1980s—Larry had recently published *Write For Your Life,* a kind of inspirational guide for aspiring writers as well as for those who had, for a variety of reasons, lost their voice or their direction; he was touring the country with his "Write For Your Life" workshop intended to spread the word. I no longer remember how I heard about the workshop. It sounded like something I would have done anything to avoid, with my scathing intellectual skepticism and contempt for anything that sounded like self-help. No matter. Something called to me, and I signed up.

Eager as ever to be one step ahead, I read Larry's book in the days before the scheduled weekend. It did nothing to reassure my inner skeptic, who is always quick to identify the bullshit in others but equally reluctant to acknowledge my own. I had always recoiled from probing too deeply into the life of the mind, and I was pretty sure that I was going to be asked to explore some secret places that I would quite honestly prefer to leave undisturbed. I knew from the book, for example, that we would be asked to identify the Big Lie—that mental formulation we invent to stand between our creative impulse and its fulfillment (absurd!); now that I was committed, I set about asking myself what my Big Lie could be. My intellect judged that this was a pretty childish game, but I settled on one that sounded about right: "I have no time to write."

So I showed up at Larry's workshop confident that I could ace it. I was, after all, a writer of experience. Did I not have a doctorate of literature in my back pocket? Had I not spent four years at the University of Iowa Writers' Workshop, one of the biggest, best, and oldest in the country? Had I not already published two books of poems, numerous articles, and critical reviews in national magazines? I showed up at the Hollywood Holiday Inn still not knowing quite why I had signed up or what I expected to learn . . . I knew it all, didn't I?

Sure enough, the moment came when we were invited to identify and announce our Big Lie to the group. When called upon, I had mine down pat: "I have no time to write," I said with some satisfaction at my own clarity. I was distressed, however, to see that Larry's response was a doubtful frown.

"That sounds more like a symptom than a cause," he said, and, after a thoughtful pause, he added, "Is there anything you can remember about your birth?"

My birth? There was a moment of sheer shock and panic. Even my worst apprehensions had not prepared me for this bizarre diversion. I have no idea what intuition might have guided him to the question, and the occasion of my birth could not have been further from my mind. But yes, there was something I knew about my birth: I was a blue baby, born with the umbilical wrapped like a noose around my neck. If not for the speedy response of the midwife with a handy pair of scissors, I would certainly not have survived. I passed this information on to Larry.

"Well," he said, "I have a suggestion." And he offered me an alternative Big Lie: "I have no right to be here."

The next step was for us to walk around the room and introduce ourselves to other workshop participants by our Big Lie. "Hi, I'm Peter. I have no right to be here." At first, I was unable to bring the words out of my mouth. I choked on them. They struck me, on one hand, as completely silly. And on the other . . . I broke down in hysterics. I couldn't decide if I was laughing or crying and realized that I was doing both at the same time. It was clear that the words had reached deep into some previously hidden part of my psyche, touching a truth so profound and so imponderable that my rational brain simply couldn't deal with it.

It was a truth, I soon began to understand, that had affected my life in many subtle and not so subtle ways: most obviously, I had sabotaged all those jobs in the ways I mentioned earlier. I had no right to be there. Even at the most trivial level, I was always the first to want to leave the party. While I'll freely confess that there was no instant cure afterward and that the Big Lie has persisted in raising its head in numerous circumstances since, it has been vital to know about it. That moment of insight was a kind of liberation.

For me, the story clarifies a critical point about the way in which creative people can sabotage their voice and their vision for reasons unknown even to themselves so long as those reasons remain unexplored. It reminds me that I am never disconnected from my past experience and that such moments of trauma, without my bringing them to consciousness, can control me in unwanted ways. It reminds me that, if I want to work, I need to work also on myself, that there is no need to be held hostage by old thought patterns and habits, that the work I do must be a continuing process of self-discovery. The more I can learn about myself, the greater the freedom I enjoy as a writer.

Here's another thing I learned: never be satisfied with the first answer or with the easy one. The moment I think I have it is often the moment I most need to keep digging. Answers, it seems to me, are always provisional. It's the questions that keep moving me forward into the unknown—which is where the good stuff is to be found.

REACHING PEOPLE

An Exchange

Adapted from an entry in my blog, The Buddha Diaries, dated 6/19/09, and from a response to it written by an artist friend.

The blog:
A good part of my dedication to the art of writing comes from my desire to reach people, to share some important part of myself with others. I understand now that my early career as a teacher must have been motivated at some deep level by this same impulse, but I was never a teacher in the conventional sense. I did it for years, but truthfully I never felt at ease in the classroom. Since the age of twelve, I knew I was meant to be a writer, and, as I came to admit to myself after years of unhappiness and self-delusion, classroom teaching was no more than a way to make a living. Academia was never my true home.

I have been thinking a lot recently about this book of essays—thirty years' worth, on and off—and how all of them touch on this issue in one way or another. There are so many creative people out there doing things they were never meant to do in order to earn a living. We even have a name for it: the day job. For myself, out of fear, out of a lack of belief in myself, under the strain of social pressures—or a mixture of all these—I chose education. Others have chosen different jobs, career paths, and professions perhaps for similar reasons, and it has been as necessary for them as it was for me to support the real work that could not support them.

But I have never been one to believe in the much-propagated consolation myth: "I do it for myself." No. I'm clear about this: I do it to be read. The other half of my creative process is the reader, without whom none of it makes much sense. It's my belief that the reader/viewer/listener is a necessary accomplice, a completion of the process. Creative activity arises from the desire to share oneself with others—a desire too often left unrequited, with dire consequences for the creative psyche.

Contemplating the possibility of this book, then, I had an enlightening conversation recently with a literary agent. I had sent out a few query letters describing the book and its intentions and received from one agent the invitation to give him a call. His point was clear and simple: in order to make a success of a book about surviving in the commercial world—and to reach the readers I wanted to reach—I would need to get commercial. He referred me to his Web site, which included a long, detailed questionnaire about marketing plans as a primary tool in attracting the interest of publishers. I'm no neophyte in the business, and he wasn't telling me anything I didn't already know from past experience, but I was uncomfortably reminded as we talked that a book's acceptance for traditional, commercial publication has little to do with the quality of the idea or indeed with the quality of the writing. It's really about being able to demonstrate to publishers that it has a ready-made audience out there, eagerly waiting to consume it . . . along with a system in place to ensure a successful publicity campaign and an acceptable bottom line. Publishers, like gallery dealers, are not in business to lose money.

My conversation with this literary agent was productive in that it led me to start thinking about other ways of reaching people.

He stressed, for example, the importance of having venues to promote the ideas to a variety of audiences in talks and lectures, which is something I have given a good deal of thought to in the past. It's a different kind of teaching, a kind that I have much enjoyed on those occasions when the opportunity has presented itself—a one-shot chance to tell a group of people, as I say in one of the book's essays, who I am and what I do.

The trick, of course, is to find the venues. One of the ideas that appeals to me is offering a workshop to students in fine-art and writing programs that would introduce them to the most powerful weapon in their creative arsenal: the mind. They already learn a lot about the use of the brain, the eye, the hand—the usual skills. The mind is something different. It's a tool that can famously work for you or against you, and it's most frequently omitted from the curriculum. As a result, it's too often left to its own devices and works to thwart us.

As I'll continue to insist throughout these pages, there is a simple, well-tested technique to discipline and train the mind to do those things one needs it for: to focus, to concentrate, and to generate new ideas. It's a technique whose rudiments are readily taught and easily demonstrated. It's called meditation. Given just an hour, I could show a class of students how to do it. Why not? After that, of course, it's up to them to put it into practice if they find it useful. I'd have loved it if someone had shown me how to meditate fifty years ago. Or forty. Or thirty . . .

But then, of course, I would not have been ready for it. It's not that the benefits of meditation were not widely touted back in the 1960s and the 1970s. Think of Alan Watts. Think of Ram Dass. The sad truth is that even while such writers were doing all they could to reach me with their books, I was not ready to hear what they had to say—even though their marketing could hardly have been better. That's how it goes, and more's the pity.

My artist friend Gary Lloyd's response to my blog entry that same day:

The marketing of art is the one factor that drove me out of the market, because it took away valuable art-making time left after long teaching days spent helping young and old art students develop their skill sets. The market was and still is driven by the gatekeepers of the gallery-museum complex you know so well. Creativity is driven by innovation, personal passion, and *satori*. Popularity is driven by the desire for recognition, ego fulfillment, and marketability.

If artistic concepts are relevant and unique to the furthering of what art can be—like the work of, say, Robert Irwin or James Turrell—they must be championed by writers and critics whose social and political standing within the market is already validated by the gallery-museum complex so that their critique can bolster financial investment opportunities. The Medicis of our day still determine the direction of marketing by their support and patronage.

It may be artists themselves who unintentionally collaborate in this because of their desire to share or show work and receive feedback, or because of their need for money to further their art-making activity. Many of the most well-exposed artists make work tailored to fit into venues established by the market. Certain large and shiny bunnies (Jeff Koons) or graphics (LeRoy Neiman, say) promoted in the name of popular culture are currently very marketable. These items will have a relatively short historic shelf life even if collected by the complex. Even so they are expensive to insure, display, and circulate. Museums are going broke because of this twentieth-century cycle of recognition, procurement, distribution, justification, protection, and collection.

The artists I revere most have retained their identity and the integrity of their work by doing what comes naturally rather than creating what can be sold. Art that inspires the soul and creates new ways of seeing may find that the Internet is a fine tool for bypassing middle managers and patron-driven critics in this permutation of human development. Presently, the rich collectors are protecting their diminished wealth by standing on the sidelines waiting to reinvest in the next best "thing."

Wouldn't it be a better art distribution experience if a kind of Internet clearinghouse made the playing field level by offering works to the world without the 50 percent markup the complex creates? Many artists already have excellent Web sites or studios online just waiting to be viewed if someone knows they are there. What may yet be needed is a kind of enterprise that brings them together like Amazon does. Who will make that happen?

My thoughts on Gary's response:

The gallery-museum complex sounds a bit like the military-industrial complex that has a stranglehold on the national economy and the policies that determine the direction of this country. These two institutions affect our small circles in much the same way. Does the Internet offer a way out, as my friend suggests? Depends, I guess, on how we artists use it or how we let it be used by those who want to make a profit from our work.

SEPTEMBER 11

Despair, and Why It Matters to Carry On

Adapted from an essay written soon after the September 11, 2001 attack on the World Trade Center in New York.

What could I do? The enormity of the events of that awful day left me with the empty feeling that no matter what I did as a writer sitting at my computer risked seeming inconsequential when compared with acts that sent shock waves of pain, grief, and fear through the lives of so many human beings. Even before the disaster that preoccupied my dreaming and my waking mind in the days that followed, I had been finding it hard to resist a sense of futility as I exercised the most important gift with which I felt myself to have been endowed.

I found myself thinking too often that the art of writing had come to seem a bit old-fashioned, almost quaint. Newer, faster, and more seductive media are rapidly replacing it. Besides, as a poet—which is where I started out—could I ever hope to reach more than a handful of readers? As a novelist, I could expect two or three thousand readers at best—if indeed I was fortunate enough to get a book in print—unless by some miracle I were to make it into that tiny elite whose books appear on the best-seller lists. As for being an art critic and observer of the contemporary art world, let's be honest. How many people seriously read and care about this tiny niche in the world of elite culture?

Even before the Word Trade Center outrage, my experience upon entering a bookstore was an overwhelming, physical sense of nausea. My God, so many of them, newly published! So many classics, impossible to match for their assured place in the hearts and minds of readers . . . who would be so foolish and presumptuous as to follow such a calling?

But the events of September 11, 2001 certainly served to pull this malaise into a clearer and more poignant focus. What could I hope to do after that, especially, in a world that seemed so undeniably and inalterably changed? I found myself thinking about paper—that image of paper falling from the smoke- and debris-blackened sky in a slow, white, eerie snowstorm. It occurred to me that I have always had a special relationship with that most ordinary of cultural necessities. Aside from its utility, I've always had a feel for its physical properties: its texture and dimensions, its weight and color. I've always loved the way that words take shape on paper. It has been, to put it simply, my stock-in-trade.

So in the new world of September 11 I sat as though hypnotized, watching those television pictures recording the sickening spectacle of the collapsing skyscrapers, and I saw paper everywhere. It drifted about in blizzards of ominous, apocalyptic snowflakes. It gathered in dusty, mountainous heaps of trash, extending the full length of a street and beyond, past all imaginable corners and out of sight. I saw paper crumpled, ripped, shredded, or burned into thick, black wads of sodden ember; I imagined corporate reports, calendars filled with what once were pressing business dates, proposals, financial statements spelling out wealth or poverty, email messages, pages from books in progress or from journals . . . their relevance to some actual person now irretrievably lost.

As a writer about art, I have had a special relationship with images. Paper in this new context became an image of particular significance for me as a part of a greater image. It speaks powerfully of the suddenness with which meanings can be trivialized and ambitions mocked, of the belittling ease with which destiny—by whatever name we wish to call it—can transform all human pretense of order into chaos with a casual sweep of the hand. What could I do with a string of words to match the power of such an image?

For that matter, what image could an artist create to equal the power in the journalistic photograph of a woman so gray with dust she seemed two hundred years old emerging from the toxic yellow filth of a disintegrating skyscraper? Or in the video pictures of an airliner with a full complement of crew and passengers slicing through steel and glass as though through an upright bar of butter? Or in the view of the jagged grid of steel that towers, as the sole standing remnant of the building, above a mountain of rubble? Or in the image of the woefully floating body of a man who chose death by falling over death by fire drifting with awful grace toward the plaza below?

We saw such images a hundred times, and still they exercised their gripping power. We could never appropriate them; instead, they appropriated us, seared into a place in our brain where we knew they'd never be erased.

The same can happen with words. Do you watch television? Are you done to death by the pundits with their mealy mouthings of opinion cooked up for whatever occasion presents itself? Do you listen to talk radio? Are you weary of those hosts and their callers with their peeves and gripes? Do you read the papers with their reams of words that are all to be discarded at the end of every day? And then there's the constant chatter of the Internet.

Like most everyone, in the wake of September 11, I received literally hundreds of emails and forwards. Each one of us had his or her piece of wisdom: an insight or suggestion, a protest or a word of praise for the police, the firemen, and the emergency workers. Some I read, some I erased with the click of a mouse. I had my own rant, at the time, about what those terrorists had wrought, and it went out to patient readers or perhaps was ignored and trashed. What I'm writing now, in retrospect, is a part of it: that avalanche of words . . .

I knew a beautiful young man who was working that morning on the 101st floor of one of the World Trade Center buildings.

And then, in an entirely different context, another good friend, an old friend of my own age, in his mid-sixties, died that same week following a massive heart attack.

When death comes visiting, it can be so confoundingly arbitrary, so far beyond the reach of words. You see what I mean. The events of September 11 just slapped us in the face with it. And yet, while it would be dishonest to deny that stark reality, there's still the need to step forward into hope.

So what could I do? One thing I have learned is that I can breathe. It sounds simple, even simple-minded, but I tend to forget too easily that at every moment I'm reaffirming life with this most basic act. I can watch my breath arrive and watch it leave my body. I've learned that this brings comfort, calm, perspective— even wisdom of a sort—just to sit and watch the breath and let the rest of the world go by.

In consequence of that awful day, I applied myself also to the challenge of meditating on death. I applied myself to becoming fully rather than just half aware of death's inevitability, to realizing that it has happened to every other being that ever lived, and that with greater than 99.999 percent probability, it will also happen to me. What the practice brought up first was a lot of fear and sadness and a good deal of grief. But the surprise is that gradually the unshrinking awareness of death begins to make everything else matter. It matters that I take in the next breath—and that I make it a delightful one. It matters that I look out the window and notice the last of the oranges on my neighbor's tree. It matters that I honor this very moment by being conscious of it, by not letting it slip away unnoticed.

And from this perspective, I have discovered, it matters that I write. What a relief it is to realize that it matters that I write without thought for the outcome, without attachment to publication and readership, without need for thanks; what a relief to realize that it is enough to write in simple consciousness. There's a distinct and peculiar joy in dedicating myself to setting down each word with the clear understanding that it could be the last I ever write. *That's* when it takes on meaning.

PRACTICE

Breathing Mindfully

First, sit comfortably, eyes gently closed and hands in your lap (no need for those crossed legs, but a good, straight back is essential). Bring your attention to the breath.

Watch the rise and fall of the abdomen as the breath fills and empties it. When the mind wanders, bring it back to this area, and hold it there for a good couple of minutes to start.

Then allow your focus to rise to the area around the solar plexus and spread out to the right side of the torso. Keep bringing the mind back to the breath for a couple more minutes as it watches this area. Then shift the mind gently over to the left flank . . .

Move the attention up to the heart and settle the focus there for a while before allowing it to spread out once again to fill the whole area of the chest and the entire torso. Breathing out, breathing in.

Bring the attention to the base of the throat and watch the passage of air, relaxing the muscles of the neck and opening the throat . . .

Now the head: imagine it as a sieve, with breath entering from all directions. Notice the muscles of the jaw, the lips, the inside of the mouth . . . the ears, the nose, the nostrils . . . the sockets of the eyes and the contour of the eyeballs . . . the cavity of the skull, and the brain. Take care to allow the mind to relax as you remind yourself to concentrate only on the breath.

Work the breath down the spine, breathing in between each disk on the descent, and watch it move down the right leg, to hip, to knee, to ankle, and out through the end of the toes; and the same with the left leg . . .

Bring the attention to the base of the neck and breathe into the cluster of muscles there, inviting them to relax with every out breath. Then move down the arms, right and left in turn, and out through the fingers . . .

Now watch the whole body breathe, as one, as if it were a single, giant lung, rising and falling with each breath. After a while, allow the contours of the body to melt away as you become nothing but breath . . .

WHAT TO SAY

When There's Nothing to Say

If you're anything like me, you'll have days when you wake up in the morning with that feeling of dread: when I show up for work, *I won't have anything to say.* It's an awful feeling. The ground seems to fall away from under me and in its place arises . . . *panic!* My brain takes over, accelerating to hyper warp speed and zooming off in its familiar search mode, dashing hither and yon in the sheer desperation of finding something intelligent to say: something that makes some sense, that communicates something of importance; something that will astound my readers with my wisdom and the depth of my experience and compassion; something that will contribute in some significant way to the well-being of this troubled world and those with whom I share it; something, eventually, that will validate me and make me feel good about myself. The counterpoint, of course, is this: if I don't have anything to say, I'm worse than useless. I'm a parasite. I'm a fraud. I know it's pretty stupid thinking, really. But the feeling is a real one.

So what to do about it? I've found the first thing, always, should be to take a breath. One of the best-known and least successful human responses to panic is to stop breathing—as though that helps! So it's important, I find, to sit quietly for a good few moments to restore a measure of serenity by the simple process of consciously observing the breath as it enters and leaves the body, allowing its rhythm gradually to replace the brain's hectic activity with its peculiar, calming discipline.

Breathing out, breathing in . . . When you think of it, this in itself is nothing more or less than inspiration.

That done, I have several mental strategies I deploy to get back into the process of creation. Because that's what it's about: creative work is never about saying something. It's about process. It's a dance, an interaction with medium, no matter what your medium might be: words, paint, clay, song, or musical notes. The need to have something to say is no more than an impediment we set up when we're too worried, too scared, too timid, or too mistrustful to risk letting it out and damning the consequences. (Fear, of course, is a great inhibitor. I wrote a book a while ago titled *While I Am Not Afraid*. The title was borrowed from the book's epigraph, a wonderful text by the artist Duane Michals to accompany his photograph of a male nude: "Let me write this now, / This very moment, / While I am still foolish, / Before I become sensible again / And know better; / And while I am not afraid / To say things out loud." A text, in my book, literally, to live by!)

My next step is to extend my attention to the breath into an actual meditation in which I purposefully try to nudge out all intruding thoughts and give the mind the simplest (and hardest) of all tasks: to focus exclusively on the breath itself. What happens when this tactic is successful is that the unconscious mind slips quietly into gear and keeps on driving while my brain is busy with its neutral concentration on the breath; when I open my eyes and return to the normal state of being, I find that the unconscious mind has completed a good part of the initial journey for me. I'm ready to go, and the words start to flow effortlessly.

Another tactic also requires some quiet reflection time: I sit and tell myself the story of yesterday. It's not necessarily a narrative that comes up—although it might be. Very often, though, it's a single moment, an event, a mini-epiphany that arises, perhaps one that I was simply unaware of as it occurred and disappeared unnoticed and unmemorialized into the past. It could be no more than a glance from a stranger in a crowd, the movement of a hand, the expression on a face. It could be the turn not taken, the adventure passed up in favor of the familiar route. It could be the glimmer of light on the surface of the ocean . . . Yesterday, for me, is always filled with moments rich in opportunity, in unprocessed, unrecorded matter—an abundant source of what to say.

As is, of course, the Now. Sometimes I have only to look around me. The images are there, the signs I need to follow: a photograph of my grandfather on the wall, the dog in a patch of sunlight on the carpet, the notepad on my desk with a couple of words scribbled out on it. Each moment is in itself a complex mother lode, replete with particular and inscrutable meaning, awaiting nothing but my pick and shovel to start mining it.

Just as fruitful as a resource for that first image, that first word, that first idea, is the daily newspaper. You don't even have to be looking for news. There's a surprising wealth of discrete images in the photographs, in the ads, in the texture of the words. Pages and pages crammed with stories, people, insights, problems, conflicts . . . We need not take them literally. The imagination, once it's opened up and ready for adventure, can seize on anything and run with it. What happens all too frequently is that the search for something to say is precisely what shuts the imagination down, turns it off, or freezes it into inertia. In the meantime, opportunity is right there, staring us in the face from a common newspaper—not to mention the inexhaustible resource of books and images others have created in their search.

Finally, not least, there is the resource within dreams and fantasies. I myself am not actually very good at remembering dreams, though I do believe that we can train our minds to recall where they take us in our sleeping hours. Inevitably, though, when I do remember them, my dreams create a wonderful maze of paths to follow as I write them down. Again, I'm careful not to get too attached to trying to recall every detail with painstaking accuracy. Once I'm on the path, I tend to follow where the words and images lead me, rather than the strict narrative of the dream. Once I get into it, it's the medium I trust to show me where I need to go.

Whatever strategy I choose to deploy, here's the thing: it's not only ludicrous for me to tell myself that I have nothing to say, it's also a damn lie. The more honest truth is that it's impossible *not* to have anything to say. As soon as I open my mouth, complete a gesture, perform an action, no matter how trivial it seems, I have created meaning. I have said something. My very inaction, my paralysis says something, as does my panic. So I take heart when that feeling surfaces. I remind myself that it's always possible to step around these self-created barriers and venture forth, beyond them, into the unknown, which is where creation happens. And I try to remind myself, as I start out on that next adventure, that I'm much better off if I don't have anything to say—if I don't have the least idea what I'm looking for until I've found it.

THE BANDAGED PLACE

Confessions of a Recovering Intellectual

For many years I counted myself amongst those who reject the notion of creative work as a potential source of healing. I saw both the practice and the appreciation of art as a largely formal and intellectual exercise: a game of the mind—a game capable of infinite richness, perhaps, but nonetheless a game. And I confess that, privately, I would look down on those who saw it otherwise as members of a less-informed species who lacked my superior intellectual resources.

How arrogant and wrong-headed I now see myself to have been! Perhaps it's the advance in age that has weakened my brain, but I now find myself increasingly disinterested in art that is not in some way able to help me feel more fully human; and if feeling that way is not healing, I don't know what is.

"Don't turn away," the poet Rumi wrote. "Keep your eyes on the bandaged place. That's where the light enters you."

Keep your eyes on the bandaged place. In creative work—for me, particularly, in writing—I understand this to mean probing into those areas where we are most exposed and vulnerable. I have also come to understand that being vulnerable does not necessarily mean being soft and squishy. For an extreme example, in the field of visual art, consider the sculptor Richard Serra's overwhelmingly powerful tilting arcs in cor-ten steel. These certainly put me in touch with my vulnerable humanity if I dare to walk in their oppressive shadow—even though this requires the sacrifice of my judgments about the ego of an artist who presumes to impose his vision in so imperious a way. The massive structures remind me of a "bandaged place" in my own psyche: the sense of my own smallness, my petty envy of those who manage to be grandiose, those who speak with a loud and clamorous voice, those who defy the decorous rules of etiquette and self-effacement that too often constrict my vision. I am equally sure—though without needing to explore the psychological reasons for it—that these grandiloquent statements spring from some "bandaged place" in the artist's psyche, too. It reveals itself with eloquent sufficiency in his work. In this context, his humanity speaks secretly, intimately, to mine, and healing of a kind takes place for both of us: for Serra in the making, for myself in the experiencing of his work.

Nor by this sense of vulnerability do I allude to anything like the fuzzy sentimentality of contemporary pop psychology. Go back to Shakespeare. No mealy-mouth there. Go to Michelangelo's *David,* or his *Moses.* How much about masculinity—strong, yet deeply vulnerable and perishable—can we learn from spending time with these two splendid carvings in seemingly immutable marble? How much about youth and age? How much about human resilience and fears about our own fragility? How much soul healing do we experience in their proximity?

Keep your eyes on the bandaged place. How much I wanted to avoid seeing my own, and for how many years! Not long ago, inspired by a passage in Tara Brach's book, *Radical Acceptance,* I started making a list of them—those lessons about myself and the world that I had learned in childhood, beliefs I mistook for unquestionable truths simply because I had lived with them for the better part of my life without ever stopping to question them. A sampling: that the sometimes-painful realities of life should be suppressed in favor of polite appearances, and that embarrassment must be avoided at all costs. (Remember that hilarious—and for me, tellingly poignant—speech in *A Fish Called Wanda*, when John Cleese, arch-Brit, is caught butt-naked in the apartment of a total stranger, and describes the Englishman's agonized fear of embarrassment to that deliciously shameless, taunting American wench, Wanda, played by Jamie Lee Curtis? That particular lesson was never, ever to risk looking foolish.) It took me years to unlearn a number of similar lessons: the so-called truth that all problems in life can be solved by the application of rational thought and action; that others always come first; that if you leave the smallest chink in your emotional armor, someone will soon pierce it to inflict painful injury, so tighten up, protect yourself well, and let no one get too close.

These are among my own personal lessons, all learned to perfection. But none of us, I think, are spared them: children are terrific sponges, they learn easily and well. They sop it all up and soak it in, without the benefit of critical judgment. You may not share my lessons, but you will have your own. We carry them around with us and—without the benefit of continuously vigilant mindfulness—respond to the events of our lives reactively, according to the untrustworthy dictates of those old, false beliefs. It's instructive sometimes to pause for long enough to make a list of them, as I did. What are the messages I received from the adult world when I was growing up? How many of them do I allow to color my perception of the world today, and how do they show up?

One natural impulse is to pretend they don't exist: they may well be associated with profound pain, or shame, or grief, and—as we have all likely learned, now that a half-century of twelve-step teachings permeates our culture—denial is too often the better part of valor. The problem for us creative people is that when we try to shut the old patterns out, they respond by shutting us down without our knowledge or consent. No matter how casual or innocently unintended, a father's suggestion that we're dumb or lazy clings to the inside of our head like gum on the underside of a school desk, sabotaging every effort to escape what we believe to be our stupidity or sloth in later years. If we're taught early to believe in our insignificance in the important world of grown-ups, we may well manifest that belief by limiting our adult work to trivial pursuits or to minimal expectations of success. Conversely, a sense of over-importance can lead to flatulence and bombast.

These are what I call the "bandaged places": the wound is patched but not yet healed. We protect them by covering them up, forgetting that generally a wound will heal much faster if we expose it to the air. But when we learn to keep an eye on them, as Rumi suggests, we begin to discover their positive effects. They turn out to be our allies rather than our enemies.

This is where the meat is—and it's not what is taught in the schools. What's taught in the schools, for the most part, continues to be the tough line: intellectual discipline, competition, control of the medium, and a hard head for business. What is too readily passed over in our creative arts departments—perhaps because it requires much soul-searching to teach—is the heart of the matter, the vulnerable part that faithfully pumps the life blood. Why do we do what we do in a world that is increasingly inhospitable to the work of all but a fortunate few? The only convincing answer I've been able to come up with for myself is expressed in the formulation I keep coming back to: it's what I have been given to do. My work comes out of an inner need that is too compelling to ignore without serious consequences to my health and happiness, not to mention the health and happiness of those around me.

If I find myself paying more and more attention to the bandaged places these days, it is because I realize more and more that the work of writing is to find out more and more about my own humanity and to share it more and more with others. As

Rumi's wisdom tells us, and as the singer Leonard Cohen reiter-ates in his marvelous, melancholy "Anthem": "There is a crack, a crack in everything. That's where the light gets in." And the more I'm able to find my own wounded places, deep inside, and let the light in to illuminate the shadows, the more I am able to communicate with others: it's in our anger, in our pain, and in our grief—and our joy—that we find common ground. So I aim to write the most intimate, personal words I can, in which everyone can find a piece of him- or herself.

And in shedding light in the inner darkness, I'm also more likely to discover what has been holding me back. In working closely with writers and artists over the years, I have come to understand that I share this experience with others. Without our knowledge or permission, and absent our mindfulness, those bandaged places can impose their limits on what we have to say or how we say it. Do we deserve to command attention or respect? Only if we believe we do. How many of us have been reduced to silence, not by our lack of creative potential but by some hidden inner fear that puts its chokehold on our ability to speak? I remind myself, always and often, about that umbilical cord.

That brings me to one other lesson I learned in childhood. It came in the form of an adage that is not heard too often these days but was much bandied about in the days of my youth: "Little children," the saying went, "should be seen and not heard." It's an absurd cliché, on the face of it, but one that I heard repeated often enough—even though jokingly—to accept it as a truth: I should not be heard. So I remained quiet for much of my life. It was only with the realization of that lesson's lurking presence at some deep layer of the unconscious mind that I came to understand so clearly that I need to speak out loud and unashamedly.

When the silence returns, as it inevitably will, along with the self-doubt and despair that accompany it, I find it helpful to remember to keep my eye on the bandaged place and to remember that this, too—this silence—is the source of power. It's where the light enters me. At such moments, I have learned that the best thing is to sit quietly, to breathe, and to remind myself of the origin and of the workings of the reactive pattern. Once I have brought this understanding clearly into consciousness, it will surely loosen its grip. I can get back to work.

ON BEAUTY

Never Surrender

Adapted from an essay originally published in Artscene, *November, 1990.*

It was some years ago—long after its dismissal from serious art discussion and long before it became acceptable again—that I was foolhardy enough to use the word *beauty* in public. The context was one of those panel events with artists, critics, museum curators, and the like convened to discuss the return to favor of geometric and reductive abstraction—as though they had somehow been in exile from the art scene in the days since their arrival in twentieth-century art. I credit myself normally with a measure of tact, knowing what to say and what not to say in polite society. But in this case, I suppose I just couldn't help myself; the word popped out spontaneously before I was sensible enough to catch it: "Well," I must have said, "shouldn't we be mentioning something about beauty here?" or something equally inane.

I realized as soon as it was out that this was the Wrong Thing to have said. There was an embarrassed silence, followed by the kind of nervous titter you'd expect if somebody uttered the word *fuck* at a tea party hosted for the bishop by the vicar's wife. There ensued some earnest discussion about what did the word mean after all? Was it not too inclusive? Too general? Too subjective to be of use in any informed dialogue in our own enlightened time? Besides, was it *relevant* (another of those words that had its day and soon faded out of parlance)? Did beauty matter any more? Had we not all grown out of that childish need for a pleasing superficial appearance?

In the lexicon of then current art lingo, beauty was pretty much taboo. You could say it as much as you wanted so long as you didn't really mean it. You could walk into a gallery, for example, glance around the walls, and casually tell the dealer—even the artist—"Hey, this is beautiful stuff" without fear of offense. As in, "You like my cat?" "Oh yeah, she's beautiful." Or, "You heard how she responded when he told her that?" "Oh yeah, that was beautiful."

Okay, I was a little bit hip. I knew the word was debased and that there were good reasons for its debasement—well-argued aesthetic reasons. Two centuries earlier, the Romantics had already begun to throw out the studied elegance of their Neo-classical predecessors, insisting on individual over general truths, the particular streaks on the tulip rather than its tulip-ness. Nature was what the poet or the artist perceived, not the external norm. Beauty, as the cliché had it, was in the eye of the beholder. The nineteenth-century French poet Charles Baudelaire put it this way in an imagined dialog in the prose poem, *L'Etranger: "La Beauté? Je l'aimerais volontiers, déesse et immortelle."*—"Beauty? I'd love her gladly, if she were goddess and immortal." Turns out she's not. She stands with her feet planted firmly in the mud along with the rest of us.

Then, early in the twentieth century, such artists as Picasso and Braque began to make paintings that were beautiful by no one's standards—pictures that looked awkward, clumsily painted, unattractive in palette, and raw. Around the same time, music began to sound cacophonous and inelegant to the ear.

In the real world, too, given the atrocities of the "war to end all wars," beauty must have seemed in sadly short supply. Serenity was shattered; the lingering hope for peace amongst the people of the world (and, so it seemed, their belief in order in the universe) gave way to the apprehension of meaninglessness and chaos; and the dreadful, unbeautiful events of the Second World War improved things not at all. For the artist to be making objects of beauty in such a world was not only to regress sentimentally into a bygone past, but also to fly blindly and naively into the face of current history. In this context, as the contemporary French poet Yves Bonnefoy loftily wrote, *"l'imperfection est le cime"*—imperfection is—what? The goal, the summit, the height of achievement. On this side of the globe in the 1950s, consider the glorious, sometimes tragic imperfections of abstract expressionism, in which some have seen a transatlantic echo of French existentialism.

Today, having stumbled in upon the twenty-first century in our usual mindless way, we are witness to the continuing, ignoble spectacle of confrontation between the greedy and the needy, of the assault on natural beauty in the name of human progress— and not least, the appropriation of creative talent for commercial purposes. The powerful artifacts of—at least superficial—beauty today are made all too often not to put heart and soul in touch with some eternal truth, but rather to seduce and to deceive. Open up a popular magazine like *Vanity Fair* and spend a few moments looking through the innumerable glossy pages of advertisements, beautifully photographed and impeccably designed. No wonder so many of our younger artists have been reduced to ironic shadowboxing with the power of the media. No wonder they feel the need to stick a finger in the eye of a culture that worships glitz and glamour.

Yet the word *beauty,* no matter how debased, continues to retain some meaning and appeal for me. Perhaps what it needs is to shed some of its associations with pure physical appearances and instead reestablish its connections with other equally subjective but related values which are in short supply these days: astonishment, joy, and awe, for example.

Since the moment of embarrassment that first provoked these thoughts, of course, the word has been provisionally reinstated. Fine. I'm glad about that—though who knows when it will be thrown out again. The moral of the story remains relevant. All too frequently we allow the fads and fashions of others to define the ways in which we make art and the ways we talk about it. But the act of creation, as I understand it, is in part a gesture of freedom. It's a way of leaving some no longer needed part of ourselves behind, of casting off just one more link in the chains that hold us back.

So it's not beauty for its own sake that I particularly want to make a case for here. What's damaging is not a single word or concept, but our apparent willingness to allow that word or concept to be taken hostage by those who know no better than us in order to empower themselves with it; because once we start to believe in these self-appointed gurus, our work becomes restricted, hide-bound, obsessed by the fear of transgressing someone else's rules.

The artists I most admire and to whom I most frequently return for inspiration are those whose work defies the received wisdom of the mainstream of their day, who pursue their particular vision even at those times when it is least endorsed by current critical thought. I think, for example, of painters like Giorgio Morandi, whose small, highly idiosyncratic, quietly passionate, always attenuated still-life studies have only tangentially to do with the endless art movements that swirled around the artist in the grand sweep of modernism; or Balthus, whose haunting, subtly erotic figurative studies defied the pressures of contemporary convention and explored instead the intimate psyche of an obsessive and reclusive human being; or Agnes Martin, or Alice Neel . . . The works of artists such as these remain an always-inspiring mystery to me, the keys to which are locked forever in the enigma of the paintings themselves. It's useless to go looking for their rationale in the critical theory of the day. And yes, I'd argue anytime that their paintings are, quite simply and inarguably, beautiful.

If such beauty is at once humbling and awe-inspiring, I'd argue further, it's because it reminds us of the ephemeral place we occupy at the intersection of infinity and eternity. Our astonishment and pleasure are immeasurable in the encounter, as is our fear, since we are lifted out of the bodies that weigh us down to the Earth. We say, "Yes," because we have forgotten, for the moment at least, to demand answers to questions like "What?" and "Why?" and "How?" Buckminster Fuller said once, "When I am working on a problem, I never think about beauty. I think only how to solve the problem. But when I have finished, if the solution is not beautiful, I know that it is wrong." Perhaps that's it. Beauty is a way of coming up with something to which we assent immediately and absolutely, something that is incontrovertibly right, whether the rightness has to do with metaphysics or with physical reality, with social justice or with personal freedom, with mathematics or, perhaps eventually, with love.

So whenever I find myself kow-towing to convention or pausing as I write to wonder whether what I have to say is sensible, appropriate, acceptable, I think of the word *beauty*, and I remind myself to trust my own intelligence, my own vision, and my own intention enough to give them the freedom they demand and to take the risk.

I Am Not a Critic

Adapted from the essay first published in Artscene *titled "On Writing About Art," September 1991.*

Let me begin by reaffirming an intention I declared several years ago: I will write no more reviews. Having written scores of them over the preceding thirty years—Really? Really!—and having seen them published at various times in most of the major art publications, I came to understand just recently what many readers likely knew long before I did but were too polite to tell me: I am not a critic. In fact, I had always felt uncomfortable with the soubriquet, even when I was introduced as such at some art event. I took care instead to refer to myself as an art writer, or some such weaselly term.

Still, I can't deny that I chose for many years to wear the critic's mantle and that I made valiant efforts to look as though it fit me. In writing reviews, I thought, I should really carry that responsibility and live up to what I thought a critic ought to be: a person with extensive knowledge of his subject, possessed of a discrimination above the ordinary, having a sound theoretical aesthetic base from which to make—and justify—his judgments, and familiar enough with the art of writing to put his thoughts down with precision and clarity. It took me a good long time to come to my epiphany and to make the choice to cast that particular mantle aside.

It happened without fanfare: a review I had submitted in response to a request from a New York publication sparked an exchange of emails with the magazine's new reviews editor. They were looking, she said, for something more "blatant." Yes, that was the word used. I replied huffily, with the click of a mouse, letting her know that I don't do blatant. Well, she asked next, could I not do something along the lines of an additional adjective or two? A "brilliant" here, or an "abysmal" there, she meant, to indicate what I actually thought about the show? I thought my review had done exactly that.

I'd had different, even conflicting thoughts about what I'd seen at the exhibition in question. My response to it had been a subtle exchange between head and heart, and I had wanted, in my review, to say something about the subtlety of that exchange. I had brought with me no latest theory about painting, no set of standards by which I could measure out the paintings' quality or their relevance to current discourse. I was actually not the least bit interested in proclaiming them good or bad—or anything in between. I was interested in the subtlety of my entire reaction, an integration of body and feeling, mind and spirit, and in using my own art—writing—as a medium though which to give expression to that complexity.

True, throughout my thirty years in the role of art critic, I had frequently been through the agony of self-doubt. I had questioned my qualifications: my education has been in literature, not in art. I had next to no knowledge of art history, in which I had never taken a single course of study; and still less in visual aesthetics or contemporary art theory. I had once accepted, many years before, the invitation to teach a course in criticism at a major university—driven more by hunger for the pitiful salary, I regret to say, than by a passion to teach the course. The experience confronted me with just how little I knew and, truth to tell, how little I wanted to know about critical theory. I just did my best to keep ahead of the class in increments of a week at a time with agonizing attempts to read—let alone understand—the screeds of others more adept at critical thought than I.

All of this brought me to a clearer understanding of my skills and capabilities. My mind is not one of those that readily retain scads of detailed information. More often, no sooner do I learn something new than I forget it. I flatter myself that I am, at least, very good at remembering experiences. But facts, like the quasi-infinite roster of important or emerging contemporary artists, no. I can't remember their names, let alone sort them out without some actual work in front of me. I find the abstract discussion of art theory to be pretty much meaningless. In my undergraduate days and beyond, through graduate school and doctoral programs, I struggled mightily to comprehend the words of philosophers and aestheticians with reference to literature, alas, with pitifully modest success. My mind quite simply bogs down with the effort. It was the same with the vast amount of criticism that I read more out of a sense of professional duty than out of interest in what my colleagues had to say. I confess before the world that I did not understand the half of it—though I did experience pangs of guilt for disliking so heartily what I practiced myself. So it was with absolute clarity and without reservation—though perhaps decades too late—that I came to acknowledge that I am not a critic.

Instead, I have settled for another way of thinking about art writing that feels comfortable to me. I like to think of myself as a translator. I have played with this notion for quite some time now, even though it might seem an odd one when applied to writing about visual art. But I started out that way: a natural linguist, I was required to learn about translation at the age of six, when school work included the rendering of large chunks of Latin or French into English and vice versa. As my interest in poetry developed, along with my own skills as a writer, I found myself translating poetry from their French and German origins, even, in collaboration, from Japanese and other Asian languages. It was always a delight, as engaging as a crossword puzzle, and infinitely more rewarding when successful.

Translation, especially the translation of poetry, involves an act of experiential empathy, a kind of identification that requires not the suspension of self so much as the merger of self with another. It's a kind of making love, a way of opening to another and giving voice or vision to that other through oneself. It's the work of a medium. So that's what I think I do instead of criticism, except that—rather than translate from one language to another—I translate from a visual into a verbal language. It has always been a source of satisfaction to me when an artist says: "You really got it." That feels like the highest praise. And if I only manage to get one living, breathing part of it, well then, as Edward FitzGerald said about his classic translation of the *Rubaiyyat of Omar Khayaam:* better a live sparrow than a stuffed eagle.

If I write these words, it's partly for my own clarity. But I write them also for all those who, like me, have struggled for years to live up to images of themselves that have more to do with externally created labels, and to a multitude of expectations other than their own. The more we learn to integrate ourselves with our true nature and vision of the world, the closer we come to achieving the happiness and wisdom we so desperately seek. I, for one, am happy with these small flashes of wisdom that I'm granted nowadays; and, with a slowly, slowly more appropriate sense of who I am and what I'm given to do, I have chosen to release myself from the struggle to write criticism and to shed the uncomfortable guise of being a person I do not feel myself to be.

The acknowledgment that I am not a critic makes way for a different and more subtle exercise of the discernment that art and writing nonetheless require of me. Discernment derives, certainly, from critical acumen, but is less judgmental, as I see it, more open to give and take, more like a bargaining process.

For many years, that critic I did not wish to be and was not ever, I believe, at heart, would all too often turn his judgmental eye on me. I suspect that many will be familiar with this dreaded character. I used to call him The Editor. He would sit looking over my shoulder as I wrote, tut-tutting if I was putting down words that failed to meet with his approval and generally making a nuisance of himself. He was not only a mean grammar and semantics cop, but also an insufferable snob who would tolerate no deviation from his stringent standards of logic and intellectual correctness. I grew to fear his presence every time I sat down at my yellow pad with pen in hand.

Then one day, on a retreat, I found myself in conversation with a wise counselor about my battles with this annoying, sometimes paralyzing presence. "Why waste your energy fighting with this guy?" he asked.

"Because," I explained, "he's always getting in my way."

"So what's he trying to do with all his interruptions?"

The answer came with barely a moment's thought: "He's trying to stop me from making a fool of myself."

My friend let the absurdity of that sink in. Then he said, "So he's got your best interests at heart? He's only trying to help?"

That was true, I allowed.

"So perhaps it would be good to look at things a little differently," he suggested. "If he wants to help, enlist him as an ally rather than an enemy. When he interrupts at the wrong moment, all you have to do is thank him for his good advice, and ask him if he wouldn't mind coming back with it a little later."

Simple. I wonder that I'd never thought of it this way before. But I have used this wisdom frequently since that conversation, and it has continued to work well for me. My Editor and I are much better friends, now that I have adopted him as a collaborator rather than a critic. Have you tried shaking hands with yours?

"By Indirections...

... Find Direction Out"

Shakespeare, Hamlet, Act II, Scene 1

I often don't know what I've been missing—nor indeed that I have been missing it—until after I have put it down in words. Then I sometimes wonder why I failed to see it as it happened and regret the time I wasted along the way. Take, for example, my first visit to Italy. I had been to the country before but only fleetingly, and then only in the very north. This time I was enchanted. Enchanted by the people, by the food, by the art everywhere . . . enchanted by Italy. And I was amazed and somewhat saddened that I had never spent any serious time there before.

This was curious particularly because, growing up in England, I was a well-traveled teenager. I made a yearly trip to "the Continent" during the summer holidays, and I was a well-versed student of languages. I started learning French at five, Latin at six, German at thirteen. In those days, you learned your languages basically by rote, vocabulary, grammatical structures, conjugations, and declensions. *Amo, amas, amat* . . . *Faire, faisant, je fais, je ferai, je faisais, j'ai fait, j'aurais fait, que je fasse* . . . *Der, die, das, ein, eine, ein* . . . And so on. Or poems. *Maître Corbeau sur un arbre perché / Tenait en son bec un fromage* . . . You know it and you know it on time, or you get your knuckles rapped with a ruler, that kind of thing. Not the enlightened pedagogy of today, perhaps, but effective. I remember to this day great chunks of French poetry I learned at the age of six. I've forgotten my Caesar, though. I had visited Holland and Belgium, Switzerland and Austria, spent weeks and months on end in France and Spain, and had lived two years in Germany. Why not Italy?

A further digression: (Bear with me through these by-ways. I promise this will lead us somewhere in good time!) There had been two tentative experiences, both tending to discourage further exploration of that peninsular boot. On the first occasion, I crossed the Alps, like Hannibal in reverse, with a party of school chums and our housemaster—an eccentric whom we all called Tiger for reasons that remain obscure to me. Though he once caned me—I was caught smoking—he was really not that fierce. Tiger's ancient Morris convertible wheezed painfully over the mountains, only to be raided and robbed of all our possessions whilst we sat over coffee in some small town piazza, well before we reached Venice, our intended destination. We lost everything— cameras, passports, money, clothes—and turned back the same day to friendlier shores.

The second occasion was a day-trip from an Austrian campground with an irascible Irishman, the father of a girl upon whom I had cast a lustful but intensely bashful adolescent eye. My friend's father had been making home movies with his Super 8 camera and, leaving the country toward evening, had spotted a series of prominent posters which bade "GOODBYE ITALY" in several languages—a great coda, he thought, to his Italian cinematic opus. We stopped the car, filmed away, and heard loud shouts from a neighboring barracks. We returned a friendly wave and made to drive on, but soon noticed a much smaller sign, also polyglot, which had been obscured by the larger ones in front of it. I still remember the English version, word for word: "It is forbidden to express photographies, cinematographies, embossed works, or splashes." (There's the trained language memory at work, after more than fifty years.) The military men charged out of their barracks armed with submachine guns and escorted our party in a less than friendly manner to the nearest town where my Irish friend and I spent the next few hours under interrogation—and in between times in the only locked cell I have ever sat inside of—before we finally managed to persuade the authorities to release us, with the loss of no more than numerous feet of Super 8 film and a volatile Irish temper.

Hindsight makes it clear to me now that the otherwise surely excellent education I'd received at the public (read "private"—this was England and in England, for reasons best known to the English, private schools are "public") boarding school that I attended, had been almost exclusively linguistic, literary, and analytical. There were studio art classes, for sure, but with a teacher so pathetic and ineffectual that my usual practice was to escape through the classroom windows and head off into the bushes for a forbidden Woodbine cigarette. (Woodbines came in tens in a small green packet. They were very short, thin, and—the reason for my choosing them—very cheap. They were the reason, too, for that caning I received from Tiger.) The left brain was deemed worthy of education, it seems, but the right was not—though, come to think of it, I also don't recall a single art history class, and, while names like Michelangelo and Leonardo must have been familiar to me, it was surely as leading Renaissance intellectuals rather than as painters. In this and numerous other ways, it has been become increasingly clear to me in recent years to what extent my apprehension of reality has been rooted in linguistic structures; it's not surprising in this context to remember that language was what eventually brought me—by yet another indirection—to discover my empathetic relationship with art.

I did not realize it at first, but in retrospect, it's clear that even my very first book, a slim collection of poems called *Aspley Guise,* was striking in its insistence on the visual and tactile memory.

Seen through a child's eye, the central, recurring images were markedly physical: stained glass, raised tombs and brasses, the medieval architecture of the country church in the village where my father served as rector. When I finally came around to writing about contemporary art—the medium in which I have most frequently worked and to which I owe the better part of my reputation as a writer—it was in response to a gallery installation that had profoundly shocked me; and it took the form of an extended poem, later published in collaboration with the artist, as an artist's book.

So if I had never been to Italy—to return, as the French say, to my sheep—it was perhaps also in part because there seemed to be no particular call to go. To get your language fix, you can pick up a book anywhere and dig in, and I think it may never have occurred to me that I was missing something in not actually *seeing* the Renaissance. Nor that it might not be available in digested or encyclopedic form, as in a library or at the museums I dutifully visited. If *Aspley Guise* today suggests that my mind had always been apt to apprehend the world by visual means, that aptitude went for many years—not neglected or unused, surely—but certainly unrealized at the conscious level. I must have been paying attention with my retinal faculties, but I never understood the extent to which my consciousness was shaped and changed by visual experience.

So I had passed my own mid-century mark before I went to Italy and was overcome by the intensity of it. I started in Rome, with half-remembered bits of Roman history, Caesar's chronicles read in Latin, along with those fictional reconstructions from *Quo Vadis* to *I, Claudius* and found myself standing outside the Senate. The Temple of the Vestal Virgins, for God's sake! The Coliseum . . . All places which, until that moment, had existed in my mind only as literary constructs. I was in Rome where, from virtually any vantage point, the centuries stack up in a glorious three-dimensional assemblage of richly textured stone: pre-Christian, Romanesque, Medieval, Renaissance, Baroque.

One rainy morning I stood in line to get into the Vatican Museum and, once inside, made my way through the gathering crowds to the Sistine Chapel. Inside the chapel, the tourist throng occupied every square inch of floor space. We stood there, hundreds of us, shoulder-to-shoulder, gaping up at the walls and the high ceiling, with attendants on loudspeakers every few moments reminding us to move on, to make room for the next contingent of visitors backing up at the entrance. Hardly optimal viewing conditions, you'd say. Yet for those few uncomfortable, claustrophobic minutes, it seemed to me that the artist himself was in some strange way present, then and there, and that I was intimately in touch with this one man's peculiarly sensual—no, fundamentally sexual—understanding of the true source of both human longing and human spiritual aspiration. I heard him asking me to look into my own heart and acknowledge that part of him in myself.

None of this I would have known had I not chosen to put it down in words. Which brings me back on track, to where I've been heading through this maze of indirection: to an old adage, a bit of a chestnut, really, but one that has served me well through a good forty years of writing. I learned it from a friend back in the 1960s, the British poet Michael Dennis-Browne, and I continue to repeat it as often to myself as I do to those with whom I get to talk about making poetry or making art: "How do I know what I think 'til I see what I say?" It's the essence of process; and the work of the artist, for me, is nothing if not process. It's all about finding out what I had missed until now, about following the words until they lead me where I didn't even know I wanted to go until I got there. It's all about play, about the interplay between the human senses and the human heart, about the dance—or sometimes, more painfully, the hand-to-hand combat—with medium. It's about learning to listen before saying; it's about not knowing and the adventure of finding out.

So in my own work, I'll continue to let the words flow where they will, and I'll follow where they lead—even though they lead me through unexplored and unexpected byways, as they have just now done. They have guided me well thus far. I've learned to trust their wisdom, and they never stop coming. That's the joy of it.

ON DISCIPLINE

It occurs to me that our culture does not much encourage us to honor discipline, much less to practice it. We grow up believing it to be the enemy of creativity and an obstruction to our imagined freedoms. While we grudgingly acknowledge its value—for others, chiefly—it is not something we embrace with enthusiasm in our own lives. This is a shame, because it's discipline alone that can teach us to prioritize, to strategize, to persist, and to achieve.

Each one of us faces multiple choices in our daily lives, and we do not have time for all of them. I don't know about you, but for me the days are more likely to seem too short than too long. Between the chores, the errands, and the necessities (like eating!), it's often hard to find the time to do those things I actually want to do; and there are so many of those that I won't get any of them done unless I make some choices. I have to prioritize, to choose among them those that are the most important. It's a kind of mental triage, much better performed mindfully than when I allow pure circumstance to make the choices for me.

Once the choices are made, it's a similar practice of discipline that I need in order to strategize the implementation of my plans. Without some basic organization, things tend to go rapidly awry. I will need the basic materials; I may need to enlist the support of others who may be more reluctant than I to see it through. I will certainly need to organize my thoughts or—if I prefer not to start out with the thoughts but rather develop them along the way—at least find that starting thread that will lead me where I want to go and determine the time and place I need to make it happen.

Of all the disciplines involved, however, I think persistence is the most important and possibly the most difficult. There will inevitably be many distractions and many disappointments as I work, any one of which can weaken my resolve: the telephone rings, and it's an important call that needs my immediate attention; the dog throws up on the carpet; the bills have not been paid; the leaves need sweeping outside in the garden; or the work is proving harder than I had imagined; the words won't flow the way I want them to; what I thought at first was an excellent start turns out to lead me nowhere. I begin to worry about whether I've said it right, about how I might be judged by others.

I can soon find myself in a stew that only persistence can help me out of. Persistence is a discipline, too. It's a rejection of every distraction and excuse that comes along and a return of my attention to the task at hand. It's a refusal to be deterred from the purpose I have set myself, a quiet insistence on the pursuit of this particular goal. If I don't have it and put it into practice, I can forget about achievement. I won't be going anywhere.

In order to overcome these challenges, some mental training is necessary. Discipline does not arrive of its own accord; it does not come naturally. On the contrary, it's hard earned, and it's a quality that's nurtured too little in our schools today.

How to acquire it? Put it into practice. The simplest and the hardest way I know—and the most effective—is meditation. It's simple because it asks for nothing more of me than time to sit and pay attention to the breath, which most of us have in ample supply for free. It's hard because it asks for time and patience. The mind wanders. That's its nature. The discipline consists in bringing the mind back to the breath, time and again, until it learns to stay put, focused exclusively on the breath.

A perhaps even harder part of the discipline that meditation teaches is just to show up. Most of us have trouble doing that. We have trouble showing up to our work because we are too busy, or too lazy, or too fearful of what might—or might not—happen if we do. Sadly, we fail to show up to our lives for the same bad reasons. Learning to show up every day for meditation, without excuses, without question or prevarication, is for myself a proven way to put discipline into practice.

And—take it from one who has been working at it for some fifteen years—it's always just as simple, and it never gets any easier. But, once learned, the art of discipline rewards me with more and greater benefits in life than I would be able to name. It opens the door to everything I'll ever want to do.

No

T he tiny word sounds simple enough, but for me it has
always been the hardest one to say.
No.
My every instinct rebels against it. It's cold, definitive, rejecting,
and uncooperative. It's rude. One of the many rules I was sternly
taught as a child is that it's not nice to say no, and to be nice was
the most fundamental, non-negotiable imperative.

Yet *not* to say no, in my adult life, has too often proved a lapse
that has had the opposite effect from being nice. Every time I say
yes when I really mean no, another ugly lump of resentment and
anger is added to the mass that can, without mindfulness and
careful monitoring, accumulate in the pit of my stomach, which
is where I carry it. That's certainly not nice.

I had to smile during meditation this morning. I caught myself
being so involved in thinking about not being able to say no that
I couldn't say no. The practice when the busy mind takes over, I
have been taught, is first to recognize that it has wandered and
then to say, Not now. I have developed a modest skill in dealing
with intrusive thoughts in this way. But this morning . . . Not a
chance. I couldn't say no.

What happens when I can't say no is that I never get to do
what I intend to do. This morning, I couldn't get past the racing
thoughts and into the meditative state that would have been far

more rewarding. It was what I'd intended when I first sat down, but I never got there.

I know there's the familiar psychotherapist's jargon for this phenomenon—and, like all jargon, aside from being annoyingly trite, it also happens to describe an important truth. In this case, the word is *boundaries*. Nice people find them difficult to observe. We feel compelled to say yes to everything in order not to offend others or fail to meet up to their expectations, even—no, especially—those we love. It's the "yes, dear" syndrome.

If I find it hard to say no to others, it's equally true that I find it hard to say no to myself. That extra helping of mashed potatoes? Yes, please! Lie in, forget the meditation, get to work a little later? Sure, why not? I indulge my cherished vices with unseemly relish.

But no is a vital word to master if I'm to get the essay written, if I'm to get the book completed. Demands and requests flow in from all directions constantly. There's the trip down to the market for a fresh carton of milk. There's the picture to hang, the yard to be watered, the malfunctioning lamp to fix.

Well, no.

There's that call for help with someone else's project. They need your expertise, your advice.

No.

There's the friend who just needs a few minutes of your time. The editor who calls to offer you a juicy article.

No, thanks.

It never ends. Every yes gobbles up my time and energy and keeps me from what I want to do, and every no makes me feel bad for being selfish and ungenerous. Every yes leaves me feeling popular, friendly, likeable, wanted. Every no leaves me feeling that one person less will love me.

The surprising truth, though, is quite different. Saying no when I really mean it, and yes *only* when I mean it is not merely satisfying to myself. It means that others know where they stand with me, that they can take my word at its face value. That's important, too.

PRACTICE

A Quick and Easy Meditation

I find it useful to stop what I'm doing from time to time and take a moment to get recharged. I've been sitting at my computer all morning. The body needs a little exercise. I stretch. I take the dog out to chase his ball. The mind, too, needs a little exercise.

Sit. Breathe.

Once focused, imagine a line connecting the base of the torso with the molten core at the center of the earth. Breathe in that smoldering energy. Flood the whole body with it, head to toe, fingertip to fingertip.

Now imagine a line connecting the crown of the head with the furthest point imaginable in the universe. Breathe in the crystal-clear light. Flood the whole body with it, head to toe, fingertip to fingertip.

Now allow the two to merge, the fiery energy and the crystal clarity, flooding the whole body, head to toe, fingertip to fingertip.

And let it go.

STUFF AND NONSENSE

T hings are a drag. The lighter I travel, the further and faster I go. Who could argue with that? And yet . . . I confess that I'm addicted to owning things. I love my house, hard-earned and paid for over many years. I love the little beach cottage that the equity in that house allowed my wife and I to buy, many years ago when such things were relatively affordable. I love the artworks that we have on our walls—some of them bought, some inherited, some of them reaching us as generous gifts from artists. I love the collection of early twentieth-century American art pottery that we started acquiring back in the early 1970s when you could still pick up a treasure at a swap meet or garage sale for ten or fifteen dollars. (Not any more. These days, the prices at swap meets tend to reflect what somebody *thinks* something *might* be worth, just in case it happens to be valuable.)

So I'm no ascetic when it comes to the possessions department. I sometimes complain about the clutter and sometimes admire those who manage to live in zen-like privation and whose home environments are characterized by bare and gleaming hardwood floors, a vase here or there, a chair or two, a gong. There are times when such clarity and freedom from the thinginess of life seems enviable. Mostly, though, I'm more than content with the way things are in our household—and that might frankly be described as abundant. We own a lot of stuff.

But when you think about it with any seriousness, the fact of death alone makes nonsense of the notion of ownership. Whatever I believe I own is inarguably no longer mine when I leave this world. As the cliché cheerfully has it, "you can't take it with you when you go," and leave this world we all must, willy-nilly, and likely not at a moment of our choosing. Whatever I thought I owned in my lifetime will be left behind for others to inherit, distribute, donate to charity, dispose of, or destroy.

What of the things I think I own while I'm still alive? My money can be taken from me at a moment's notice—by theft, by accident, by reversal of fortune, by bankruptcy, by lawsuit. My house, with all its furnishings, its books and pictures, its electronic gadgets? They can all be taken from me in the flash of a fire or the cataclysm of an earthquake. Even my identity, these days, can be stolen at the drop of a hat—or rather, at the click of a mouse. So what is mine, I'm left to ask? My property? My little patch of land? My body? Even that most personal of possessions is subject to the aging process, disease, death, decay.

One of my favorite mantras, recalled at moments of distress, crisis, or despair, is this one: "This is not me, this is not mine, this is not who I am." I find it truly liberating. Once, then, I realize that I myself own nothing, I begin to question the whole idea of ownership.

An "ownership society"—as proposed by the U.S. President George W. Bush of dubious reputation—is one where we all get attached to the deluded belief that we actually do own something, in which we will do whatever it takes to hold on to what we think we have, and in which we will strive mightily to get more of it. When I get more of some material thing, it means, necessarily, that some other person will have less: unlike such immaterial qualities as good will, love, and compassion, material things are a finite resource. Ownership, then, can lead only to possessiveness, greed, and strife.

What's the alternative? I remember fondly the thinking of my late parents-in-law, Michael and Dorothy, who were art collectors of some note, though on a modest scale. They were not among those high-end acquisition demons who amass a fortune's worth of blue chip masterpieces and drop a few million at the auction house without turning a hair. No, they simply loved the stuff. Art filled their home. But like many of the collectors I've had the good fortune to meet in my years as a professional art writer, they considered themselves not owners, but rather temporary custodians of the pictures they collected. They felt privileged to have managed to gather the works around them for a while, but remained always aware that they belonged to a much wider human public than themselves, and would eventually return to it.

This seems to me an eminently healthy attitude toward what we think is ours: we are in some way blessed to have it in our custodianship for the time being, but must know that it will all flow away from us in the same great flux of life that brought it to us. To the "ownership society," then, I'd prefer the notion of a stewardship society in which we would all count our blessings with gratitude and value those things we are given to enjoy in the full realization that they are not truly ours, that we must be fully prepared to let them go.

I believe this attitude, if put into practice in our daily lives, could make us all more understanding of each other, more generous, more human. At the social and political level, I'm well aware that there are many who will scoff at such a notion and label me an idealist, a socialist, or, worse, a communist. I'm not that. I don't believe in trying to enforce some ideal of equality on the huge diversity of humankind that lives on the surface of this planet Earth. But, by the same token, it seems to me even more wrong-headed and absurd to propose ownership as the moral and political principle that will benefit us all, bringing us closer to each other and to individual fulfillment.

So what does all this mean for artists who devote their lives to making things? Is there not some measure of doubt involved in adding, daily, to the mountains of stuff that already clutter up the world? There are artists I know who feel much the same as I do when I walk into a bookstore: they worry over their own proliferating racks and cringe when they walk into the back room of a gallery, crammed floor to ceiling with the work of other artists. Museums are already overflowing with the works of art they have acquired in the past couple of centuries by gift or purchase. I wonder what percentage of their holdings remains stored out of sight in warehouses and basements. Ninety? More? It must be huge. I sometimes have this image of a once-spinning globe, stalled in mid-orbit by the sheer ballast of all this stuff with which we are continuing to load it down. (And I'm just talking about the good stuff. How about all the genuine rubbish we discard? That's another nightmare!) And artists keep churning it out, because what else can they do? They're artists.

Will there come a Big Brother day when art-making will be forbidden to all those except for those few selected by the cyborgs in charge? Will producing another object be punishable by surgery to the right side of the brain? I hope not. Yet here I sit, working away at my plan to produce yet another book to add—if I'm so lucky—to the bookstore shelves, as I've said before, if only because it's what I have been given to do.

HEY, WAIT A MOMENT

One Hour/One Painting

Everything sizzles by at baud speed these days—and I'm not just talking about the Internet. Summer arrives and is gone in what seems like the inside of a week. The year barely seems to start, and it's almost over. My head reels, trying to keep track of the days, and latches on to slim little pieces of experience in its desperation. Call me busy. I keep busy being busy.

I've come to deeply distrust the notion of information—along with its enabling kissing cousin, communication. We all agreed a while ago, with a measure of self-congratulation, that this was the Information Age, and we couldn't help feeling a bit superior if we could gather and retain a little more information than the next person. That quantum more could mean the edge of privilege. It was money, power. Probably still is, in some circles, but not those I choose to move in.

Computers, we discovered, could help us acquire that edge. They could capture and store the information for us at lightning speed. (Just recently I read that Goldman Sachs is buying and selling by the nanosecond with superfast computers to increase their profits and get the edge over competitors. Obscene!) So we came to rely on these miraculous machines. I now have at my fingertips personal and immediate access to more information than I could possibly use in sixteen lifetimes.

I have communication coming out of—well, into—my ears.
When was the last time you were anywhere without a cell phone
in sight or sound? And how do you feel about that?

Even visual art—remember how it came to be all about communication, at least for one of those faddish moments that obsess
the art world for a few weeks or months? The quicker we could
absorb it, the better off we were. A visit to a gallery or museum
became a matter of taking in as much information as fast as we
could "get" the picture, read the label (for its information, of
course), and move on. Some very smart artists built careers on the
notion that if you can't beat 'em, you must join 'em. They started
making art to be seen at seventy miles an hour on the freeway
or art stripped in any number of ways of experiential content.
Smart art. Conceptual art. Art you could "get" in an instant—if
you were only clever enough to catch on.

Well, I have to confess I'm tired of having to be that clever,
if I ever was. Basically, I'm tired. My head, along with my body,
longs for the delights of respite and repose. It wants to stop for a
moment for a reinvigorating pause along the way, to empty itself
of useless information and fill itself instead with meaning. It longs
to have to know nothing at all to experience the delight of art.

Naïve? No doubt. Heresy? So be it.

A couple of years ago, I began to watch myself on my regular
gallery rounds. I began to watch others. I began to think about
the hours that must have gone into the making of a piece of art,
compared with the moments it took me to approve or dismiss it.
A piece of writing governs at least to some extent the duration of
the experience it offers: a poem or a novel has to be read in time.
Speed reading aside, there's no way I can glance at a poem, as I
can a painting, and tell myself truthfully that I have read it. But
here I was in the galleries, making judgments at a glance that
might last no more than seconds. And I used to be thought of as
a critic—an art writer.

By an odd coincidence, on the very day I sat down to edit the final version of this essay, an article by the *New York Times* art critic Michael Kimmelman appeared on the front page of his paper, which is unusual for an article about the museum experience. Kimmelman was writing about the habits of museum-goers and his observation of museum visitors at the Louvre, in Paris. "Almost nobody," he wrote, "paused before any object for as long as a full minute."

It was my own observation of this phenomenon, then, that prompted this promise that I made to myself: that I would make the conscious effort, once in a while, to sit patiently with a chosen artwork for at least an hour and give it the chance to tell me what it was about—to speak for itself, before I began to lay my judgments on it. I gave the practice a name: I called it "One Hour/One Painting," and, after trying it out for myself a few times, it occurred to me to take it on the road. I offered One Hour/One Painting sessions at a number of museums and galleries. Limiting participants to no more than twenty-five people, I had them sit with me for a full hour. No lecture. No art history. No discussion—except at the end, and then only about the quality of the experience, not about the art. Instead, I offered my guests a brief introduction to the practice of meditation and contemplation and walked them through the chosen painting—eyes closed to breathe, alternating with eyes open to see—with as few words as possible. The series met with gratifying success. There were few people, if any, who had sat for this long for anything unless a movie or a dinner party.

I offer it here, with the invitation to give it a trial run. There is no risk to life or limb. You can practice it in your own home or your studio, at any time you choose to do it. All it needs is the commitment of a single hour—you do need to be clear that you're giving yourself permission in advance to do this, so that you're not quarrelling with your decision along the way. Make the hour a gift to yourself, away from all the information and communication coming at you. (Switch off the cell phone!) You may find, as I have done, that the benefits extend much further than a single work of art.

So here's the drill (practitioners of meditation will be familiar with some parts of it already):

First, choose your picture. It should be preferably an original work of art, but it need not be a masterpiece. This is simply about learning to be available to what's there, not about the finer points of aesthetic discrimination. That can come later, if you wish. This is about allowing the eyes to function, in so far as possible, without interference from the thinking process. You can do this in a gallery, too; all you need is to request the favor of a chair or bring your own folding stool.

Begin, as always, with the breath. Close your eyes, place the feet firmly on the ground with the hands laid gently in your lap. Don't be in a rush to open your eyes: if you take a few minutes to get bodily present, adjust to the breath and empty out the mind of its prejudice and expectations, you'll be astounded by the effect when you open them up to see the painting. It can be as breathtaking as I imagine it would be to step out onto the surface of a newly discovered planet.

From now on, the process will be to simply walk around the surface of the painting. Find a focal point, if that is helpful, and work out from there. Or work from the edges, one at a time, toward the center, simply allowing the eyes to take in what's there. No questions. No commentary. From time to time, allow the eyes to close gently and to rest and refresh for as long as feels comfortable—perhaps until they get hungry again. Then feed them. Better if they're greedy!

Keep reminding yourself, when the mind begins to wander, to return the attention to the breath. It's the mind that will keep wanting to ask the questions, or answer them: What in God's name am I doing here, wasting an hour when I could be really working? How is this artist using color, or form, or pattern—and what is he trying to say? And so on. Ignore it. Get back to the breath. Allow the eyes to do the work. Notice how their small muscles change direction and focus.

It's simple but not easy to do if you're not accustomed to sitting for an hour in silence. Still, I'd encourage you to take the full hour, because that makes the effort a real challenge, and one that you'll feel richly rewarded for completing. So set the alarm clock for that hour. When it's done, you'll have the pleasure of congratulating yourself on the singular and, I'm sure you'll find, the truly delightful experience of having slowed down. "Slow looking," as Michael Kimmelman wrote in his article, "like slow cooking, might yet become the radical chic." Consider this your invitation to join the advance guard.

THE PAINTING'S EDGE

Tell Me Who You Are

Extracted and adapted from a lecture offered at a working retreat and study session for artists at the Idylwild Arts Foundation in Summer, 2009. Thanks to my friend Roland Reiss.

Good evening, and thank you for inviting me, a writer, to join in this symposium of painters. It's a privilege and a pleasure to be with you. First, let me assure you that I am not a critic. When I first made this admission in the essay originally titled "On Writing About Art" (later re-titled "I Am Not a Critic"), readers from all quarters enthusiastically applauded me. The essay spoke, I think, to numerous people who were tired not only of the flatulent nit-picking of pretentious writers out to indulge their own egos at the expense of artists, but of a cultural environment in which critical response to even serious art had become too often commercially tainted and too ingrown to do more than reflect upon its own importance. Let me begin, then, by reiterating that simple declaration: I am not an art critic.

That said, I *am* a writer, and I do write about art. Over the years, I confess to having committed a sinfully large number of critical reviews for national magazines. In my defense, however, I like to think that I use words in much the same way that a painter uses paint. I started out as a poet and, as the French poet Yves Bonnefoy once wrote, "poetry is not a *use* of language, it's a madness inside language." Or perhaps, to use a metaphor that I prefer, it's more of a dance with language. In this context, I like to think of everything I write as poetry: novels, articles, memoirs, art reviews, and yes, even what I have to say to you tonight. I would like you to think of this as a reading—a poetry reading, if you will—and to listen to it as such. After all, what else does that stuffy old word lecture mean but reading? *Lecture,* as we borrowed it from the French. Besides, my own gift is as a writer, not a speaker, and I know that the words I write evoke not only meanings, but also images, wandering associations, physical sensations, feelings, etc., and I want to take advantage of all of them as much as of any content. In "Ars Poetica," the poet Archibald MacLeish famously wrote, "A poem should not mean, but be."

MacLeish's beautiful, well-known poem reads, in part, like this:

> A poem should be palpable and mute
> As a globed fruit,
> Dumb
> As old medallions to the thumb,
> Silent as the sleeve-worn stone
> Of casement ledges where the moss has grown—
> A poem should be wordless
> As the flight of birds...

And ends with these words:

> A poem should be equal to:
> Not true.
> For all the history of grief
> An empty doorway and a maple leaf.
> For love

> The leaning grasses and two lights above the sea—
> A poem should not mean
> But be.

We could say the same thing of a painting, surely. A painting should not mean, but be.

You see before you a man who writes rather often about art, but who judges that each one of you, as a painter, knows more in the tips of your fingers about art than I can claim to know after too many years of scribbling too many words in the attempt to name it. As one witty celebrity—Steve Martin? The attribution is in dispute—reportedly said: "Talking about art is like dancing about architecture."

I'm also not entirely sure what "The Painting's Edge" might be, unless it's quite literally that place where the painting ends and the wall begins. Fair enough. But I particularly want to dissociate what I have to say from the term that is so cheerfully bandied about in art circles: the cutting edge—the next art world -ism, the direction of the future, the latest theory cobbled together by aestheticians who should have better things to do with their lives. Throughout my years as a teacher, art school administrator, and writer about art, I have been dismayed by the way in which art schools and teachers of art have increasingly terrorized their students by requiring them to kow-tow to the latest theory to come along—too many of them, it seems to me, from that haven of intellectualism across the Channel from the country of my birth.

Yes, I mean France. No offense—as we say glibly when we mean the opposite—but we English pride ourselves on being pragmatists; the French have always been an enigma to us. I'm by no means the first to observe that if you compare the two languages carefully, you'll be surprised to find that the English vocabulary is rich with words and sounds that evoke infinite variations of material detail, while the French language is much more mellifluous and immaterial, stronger in words that facilitate abstract, analytical thought. (The difference is dramatized by that mute "e" at the end of so many words in French, never quite sounded, but not unsounded either, refusing somehow to allow the word a conclusion. It's actually kind of magical. If you know the language, think of that word I used a moment ago: *lectur-e*. That last "e" drifts off into the unknown.) The truth is that I have not only been dismayed by the art schools' growing emphasis on theory, I have been befuddled, bewildered, outsmarted, and left in the intellectual dust.

Thanks to friendly relations with numerous studio artists, however, I know that I'm not alone in acknowledging that I have difficulty reconciling the art I see with half of what is published in the art magazines—or alone in being more reluctant these days to devote the time it takes to actually read this stuff. When I do open a magazine, it's mostly to browse through the pictures. When it comes to doing battle with the text . . . frankly, my poor brain recoils. Worse for me is the now familiar requirement that art students be fed this stuff and cough it back up in the form of an artist's statement, presumably so that ignorant gallery dealers, the even more ignorant public, and ignorant writers like myself will find enlightenment in the splendid theoretical and critical underpinnings the artist has been told she needs to justify her work and validate its significance to the world.

Another confession, while I'm at it: I have no pictures to show you. I was immensely impressed when I was invited to drop in on "The Painting's Edge" this time last year that the invited speaker for the evening, Christopher Knight—a man I consider to be a *real* art critic (and think no less of him for that)—declined to show more than a perfunctory couple of slides or jpegs on the grounds that these reproductions of images had really very little to do with the art he was talking about. I bow to his superior wisdom. Besides, I figure that your heads are already fully occupied by the hundreds of images you habitually carry around with you as working artists and the dozens more you have added to your collection in just this one past day. What with movies, media, and the Internet, the world is already cluttered with more images than our forebears could have possibly imagined, let alone tolerated. If you're a painter, my guess is that your brain stores these things a mile a minute, anyway. Why burden you with mine?

So what, you may justifiably be asking by this point, does this person have to talk about? The truthful answer, I'm almost embarrassed to tell you, is *myself*. That sounds like an awful presumption, but I happen to believe that this is a basic truth about all human beings and all creative activity: we do art—or writing, or any creative work really—in order to learn more about ourselves and to tell each other as much as is humanly possible about who we are. I look at your art in order to get to know more about you and your perceptions and to learn what a fellow human being has to teach me about myself and about the world in which we live.

Many years ago—I return to this story often enough to know that it holds great meaning for me—I signed up at the Esalen Institute for a workshop with an ancient wise woman, a shaman from the Mexican Huichol Indian tribe. I remember nothing else about the workshop, I regret to say, but for one of those grand Aha! moments that sometimes surprise us with a flood of pure, incontestable enlightenment—those moments when we just say, gratefully, "Yes!" Here's what this wise woman told us: unlike our Western tradition of giving a name to a baby on its first arrival in the world, the Huichols first ask this question of the new arrival: "Tell me who you are."

Tell me who you are . . .

And I realized in that moment of epiphany that this was exactly what I was about. Everything I had ever written seemed suddenly to make sense in the light of this primal purpose: to tell others who I am and how I see the world. Then, through the works of others, to find out who those others are who share this world with me and seek to make themselves known.

Tell me who you are . . . This is the essence of what I want to know when I come to look at the paintings you have made—as I have been asked to do and look forward to doing with pleasure in the morning.

Here's another lesson I once learned which has remained meaningful to me all these years. I was not only a poet in my younger days, but also a student of poetry. At the University of Iowa, while at the Writers Workshop, I took a course from a distinguished professor in Comparative Literature about Wordsworth, Coleridge, and the origins of romantic lyric poetry. These two British poets were amongst those of the period—the late eighteenth and early nineteenth century—who re-discovered the treasury of ancient Greek lyric poetry. As young men, they put together a collection of these poems in English translation in a book called *The Greek Anthology,* and I learned that these brief lyrical passages—the origin of all Western lyric poetry, really—were inscription poems, carved into the trunks of trees, on stone benches or walls. They were poems that were in a sense none other than that old "Kilroy was here" inscribed to mark the passage of a human being at that particular point in time to tell us they were there.

So here it is: I expect and want no more or less from a painting, whatever its edge might be. I don't want a lecture about art theory, and I don't need you to tell me what your intention was or what your painting means. I want it to tell me honestly who you are, and in that way to afford me the opportunity to learn more about myself. I want to be able to recognize some part of myself in what you do and thus learn more about what we share as human beings living on this precious and endangered planet at this particular moment in its history. That, is seems to me, is what makes all the work we do worthwhile.

SOME ART I LIKE

Abstraction and the Inner World

The Idylwild lecture continued.

T rue to my avowed intention to talk about myself, I will
confide two contradictory things. The first is that I acknowledge myself to be an intensely reserved and private
individual. I have a large part of me that is appalled by the thought
of being seen for who I am, that wants nothing better than to
escape the prying eyes of others and their critical judgment, that
would far prefer to run away and hide than to be seen standing
here, speaking to three score listeners who will surely see me
for the dreadful fraud I secretly believe myself to be. Perhaps
there are those of you who share this need for privacy and the
accompanying fear of exposure? I happen to believe that it's a
secret part of many creative people. It's what you might call the
Emily Dickinson part.

But then I also have what I call the Allen Ginsberg part, the
opinionated show-off, who wants nothing other than to shout out
loud and be paid attention to. This is the part of me that looks out
at the world with outrage, the part that is angered by tyranny and
injustice and acts of personal violence and war, and has an urgent
need to scream about it from the rooftops. This is the conscience
part that feels an urgent sense of obligation to my fellow-humans,

that finds it obscene to fill my belly while so many starve, to live at peace with myself while so many are victimized by war. This is the part that refuses to keep quiet and disdains the need for privacy when so many public issues demand to be discussed.

Since I have come here to talk to you about your artwork, then, it will come as no surprise that I respond to two very different kinds of painting—nor perhaps that I eventually see very little difference between the two (I will mention the second in the next chapter). I have learned to live comfortably enough with contradiction.

For my present purpose, let me tell you that I love painting that is obsessive, secretive, enigmatic, seemingly self-absorbed, mystical, concerned with the inner workings of the psyche and the mysteries of the universe, and indifferent to the material realities of the external world. This kind of painting is often—though not always of course—abstract. It is sometimes monochromatic or minimal.

I had the privilege to live for many years with a small blue painting by Yves Klein, the French artist who died at a very young age back in 1962. (Klein was known, of course, for his patented "International Klein Blue"—that dusty, pigmented cobalt blue—and for the monochromatic paintings in that intense, otherworldly color that became his trademark.) This particular painting—a gift to my wife from the artist in the year before his death—hung on the wall of the dining room in our home. Small though it was, the space it opened up to the observing eye was an infinitude, reminding us every day of the vast void that surrounds our planet, in which our lives can seem tiny, fragile, insignificant—and infinitely precious. To be seen, the painting required a deliberate act of consciousness, a kind of leap into the void (for which Yves Klein is also known, remember, in a famous photograph), an act of faith, an abandonment of the small self in favor of what I can only describe as an encounter with spirit.

That's the big picture, the grand intention of certain kinds of abstract painting. It speaks to an important aspect of who I am: my discovery in recent years of the great spiritual resource of the Buddhist teachings and their practical benefits on the path of life. Because while Buddhism offers the context of a grand, spiritual vision—a vision with which the painting of an Yves Klein, say, can resonate—it also emphasizes the importance of paying attention to the detail of mundane existence. Meditation is not first and foremost, in my experience, a search for some transcendent reality, but more a way of learning focus and concentration in the world of practical reality that surrounds us. It's the here and now, the action in the present moment that's important. Enlightenment may be the eventual goal, but the path is what we have to hand: real experience.

Meditation is also not easy. It's not the purely right-brained, bliss-out activity some mistake it for. The path the Buddha laid out is in some ways quite left-brained in its analytical precision: think of "the four noble truths," "the eightfold path," and so on. To follow the Buddhist path means, first of all, making the commitment to show up and, second, the exercise of a quite demanding discipline. To reach enlightenment, insofar as I am able, involves what for me has become a key word not only as a meditator but also as a writer: *practice.*

We've all heard that corny old joke about the tourist lost in New York City who stops to ask directions from a native: How do I get to Carnegie Hall? The answer? Practice, practice, practice. Making good paintings, like meditation, then, is a matter of doing it and doing it and doing it again . . . I was about to add "until we get it right," but that never really happens in meditation. Or, if it happens, it happens in sudden and unanticipated ways, the kind of ways you can't exactly plan for. Call it insight. Or epiphany. Or breakthrough. I imagine it can be no different for a painter working in the studio. First you show up. That's hard enough in itself.

There are always a million excuses, no? The kids. The laundry. The tax appointment. That long-delayed trip to China.

Then, when you do show up, the work begins.

Which brings me to a quite different kind of self-referential painting that I love. It's the kind of painting that is an act of meditation in itself, an obsessive attentiveness to the action involved in making it, a means the artist uses (so I imagine, because I don't do it myself) to access the deepest part of the psyche by eliminating every consideration save the making of each individual mark. I think of artists like Max Cole, for instance, or Agnes Martin, whose obsession fascinates the eye and compels absolute concentration from anyone willing to devote time and patience to following their practice. Of artists working today, I think of my friend Marcia Hafif, who works typically on monochrome panels, small or large, with at most two areas of color juxtaposed with each other, building up layer after patient layer of meticulously applied paint until she achieves the particular perfection she strives for. For the observing eye, it becomes an equally patient act of contemplation to get past the conventional need for action, drama, image, and meaning, and moving into the profundity of what I can best describe as an infinitely rich and subtle there-ness.

I love, too, to be asked to follow the action of hand or arm in a more agitated surface, to participate with my eye in the building of a particular texture, because these actions seem to invite me into the consciousness of the painting's maker. Van Gogh, of course, would be a wonderful and obvious example here— but also contemporaries like James Hayward, whose turbulent, monochromatic surfaces ask me to collaborate, in a way, in the rhythmic, physical act of their creation and through that collaboration to enter into the body-mind of the creator. The right brain, I once heard a speaker say, "learns kinesthetically from the movement of our bodies," and when I find myself responding with that kind of "Yes!" to a painting, I figure that's a part of it—the human body that we each inhabit and the movements from which we learn.

These aspects of a painting help me to actually experience a part of who that painter is and also to understand more about the relationship between mind and body: the way, if you will, the body thinks. I cited earlier that old adage from Archibald McLeish that "a poem should not mean, but be." It's this aspect of the painting's being that excites me. There's a magic to it, too: you show me how you do it at the moment of the doing, and the result is at once, like its human creator, plain to see and a total mystery.

More Art I Like

The Art of Outrage

The Idylwild lecture's conclusion.

That imperative, to "tell me who you are," is nothing less than a demand for authenticity—and authenticity can come in a variety of significant ways. If I have dwelt thus far on abstract painting, it's not because figurative and representational painting do not share some of the qualities I have been talking about, but rather because abstraction—perhaps particularly monochrome abstraction—strikes me as their most extreme, and perhaps for that reason their purest, manifestation. By the same token, though, the obsessively drawn line or the obsessively observed, recurrent pattern or image can also prove the vehicle for the kind of authentic self-examination and self-revelation I'm speaking of. Here's a poem I once wrote about a drawing by a friend, the artist Marsha Barron. It's called, appropriately enough, "Drawing."

> The line proceeds directly
> from the heart, through the hand,
> to the white surface of the paper,
> with all its awkward pauses,
> its hesitations, its sudden jolts

and turns, uncharted passages
through anger, fear, and pain;
or then, long, elegant moments
of inexplicable clarity. A spindly,
long-stemmed thing succeeds
in not quite being a flower;
a chunky, volumetric shape,
in not quite being a vase:
objects that never were, nor
will be, but in the mind's eye,
now here, on paper, startling
in outline, an inner darkness
translated with fierce precision
into the real world of here-I-am.

I wanted, in part, to explore in the poem that ambiguous ground between representation and abstraction. I used the words "from the heart" advisedly, because this, too often, is the forgotten part, the part with which our hyper-active left brain feels most uncomfortable and therefore prefers to leave unspoken or ignored. I could be wrong, but it's my impression that the word is not brought up too much in art school critiques. Yet, in my view, it's an important phrase and needs to be "at the heart" of everything a painter does.

I trust you'll understand that in talking about the role of the heart in telling me who you are, I am not advocating some simple-minded notion of sincerity. Those who follow the path of personal sincerity too often end up with nothing more than sentimental pap. I'm looking for something sterner, something more rigorous, the kind of self-examination that is unafraid to explore even—perhaps especially—those parts of ourselves we would not wish to have known, perhaps even to ourselves. It's an approach that involves personal risk and at the same time integrates every aspect of what it means to be a human being. The word for what it is I'm looking for is something more like *integrity.*

Integrity is an often-abused word, so I'll try to be specific. Another lesson from the past has remained particularly meaningful
in my life. A dozen years or more ago, I became deeply involved
in the exploration of the masculine psyche—including (by now
you'll understand) my own. I learned about the archetypes of the
lover, warrior, magician, king, and their respective *affective* qualities of compassion, intention, intellect, and creativity; I learned
how the integrated personality is one that succeeds in holding
these each of these qualities in balance. I came to understand,
too, that the fully integrated human being must further have an
awareness of the earth he stands on (the reality of the world) and
of the sky above (the field of idealism and aspiration), and that
all these qualities must come together at the center, the place of
inner wisdom, the human heart.

This is the map of the psyche that guides my own path as a
writer and a seeker after the deeper truths of human nature. So
when I speak of the integrity I'm looking for in a painting, the
aspect to which I say unequivocally "Yes!" when I see it, it's very
precisely within the balance of these qualities. I may not be able
to explain or expound upon them, but I'm never more sure than
when I see them brought together in a single work of art: the
physical, the intellectual, the emotional, and, for want of a better
word, the spiritual.

As I noted earlier, it's my belief that far too much priority has
been conceded to the intellect at this point in painting's history.
Don't get me wrong; the intellect has its place; an artist, even a
painter, would be foolish to proceed without a good measure
of technical knowledge of the medium and a firm grasp of art
history—including, as needed, the work of contemporaries. But
let's not forget, minimize, or subordinate the co-equal roles of
body, heart, and spirit.

I did mention earlier that there are two kinds of art that I
particularly respond to. I have been talking primarily about the
inward-looking, self-revelatory kind of painting that explores
the inner world. I would be remiss in closing without at least

some mention of the other kind of art that appeals to me, the outward-looking, sometimes political, often socially engaged kind of painting that wants to yell its sense of outrage to the world: if we are to be fully integrated and authentic human beings, the heart and mind both require us to be conscious of the human condition, to be sensitive to the plight of others. My own daily practice is to write the "The Buddha Diaries," which tends to be the place where I look inward to find out who I am and where I stand in my life on any given day. But an important counterpart to this work is a podcast series that I do for Artscene Visual Radio. It's called "The Art of Outrage," and it's a platform for that other, public part of me that needs to make itself heard.

We live at a moment in history when there is more than enough to be outraged about. I have few friends amongst the artists and the writers that I know who do not share my anger at the actions and inactions of those in power in recent years in response to such urgent global issues as population growth, violent competition for dwindling resources, war, famine and the threat of disease, the extinction of important and beautiful life species, and other routine abuses of our planet that threaten its very existence. I personally am angry with religious as well as political leaders in today's world, many of whom vie for power and thrive on ignorance, intolerance, and violence.

So I admire those artists who have the courage to speak out on such issues overtly and with passion in their work, despite the still powerful—though perhaps waning—influence of modernist thought that rejected such engagement. Bring on the politics, I say. Bring on the outrage. Bring on the satire and the scatological. Alan Ginsberg had it right: let's have a good "Howl"! Since my allotted time with you is about to expire, let me draw your attention to just a couple of artists working today who represent, for me, the finest expression of individual conscience among the many who make this choice.

Let me start, once again, close to home. Another of the paintings I have lived with for a number of years is a work by the artist Peter Saul. You likely know about his work, even though his name is better known to artists than to the general public. (Sadly, the art world has a way of marginalizing those who fail to follow the mainstream path, and Saul's work has consistently bucked the mainstream for the past fifty years.) His paintings are outrageous, outraged, and often unabashedly political (see his portraits of politicians like Reagan, Nixon, and Bush). He feels free to use the picture plane to explore themes of social injustice and institutional abuses like corporate fraud, police brutality, and capitalist exploitation of all kinds. And yet Saul is first and foremost a painter, as he insisted in the course of an interview I recorded with him for my "Art of Outrage" series; he paints because he has to, because that's who he is, because that's what he has been given to do. He just happens to paint what's in his heart and on his mind.

Or consider, also, the work of a younger artist, Sandow Birk, whose epic series like "The Great War of the Californias" (North and South) and "Prisonation"—paintings of all thirty-three of the state penitentiaries in California in the grandiloquent tradition of the great landscape painters of the nineteenth century—combine fantasy with satire, a profound knowledge of history with a clear-sighted critique of current social issues. Birk's "Urban Works" depict the blight of the contemporary city, from pollution and homelessness to bloody gang warfare and police brutality; "The Depravities of War" exposes the outrage of Iraq with the incisive rage of a contemporary Goya.

While the twenty-first century seems finally more open to the passionate or eclectic vision, for several decades at the end of the twentieth it took courage and an unwavering sense of purpose for artists like Saul and Birk to pursue their different path. At one time, let's not forget, it took courage simply to depict a human figure in a painting; it even took an act of courage—once painting had been definitively declared dead by the theorists and critics—to make one! The powerful sweep of modernist thinking about art made it hard for dissenters, social and aesthetic, to make their voices heard. I for one am grateful that they managed to persist.

So there you have it. I thank you for your attention this evening, and for the inspiration that your work, as painters, brings into my life. It's not an easy thing, in the cultural environment our society has created, to keep the faith, to remain in integrity with our personal vision and ourselves. It is, though, for myself as I'm sure it is for you, not really a matter of choice. It's what we have been given to do. So, bless us all; we do keep doing it, don't we?

THROUGH THE LOOKING GLASS

I fell into the blogosphere. It was, yes, like Alice through the looking glass. All the rules and expectations changed. I was quite suddenly in a different and delightful world where anything was possible.

Here's how it happened: It was November 5, 2004, the day I woke to the realization that despite his multiple, transparent lies and demonstrable mismanagement, George W. Bush had managed to retain his position as President of the United States. I was appalled. By this time it was clear that the man had led us rashly us into a disastrous war, not of necessity but of his own choosing. Katrina had not yet arrived, of course, to fully expose his incompetence, but it was already clear that the man posing as our president was hopelessly out of his depth in the most powerful office in the world. If his bullying, macho posturing in response to the attacks of September 11 had seemed, at first, appropriate to a country in a state of shock, there were soon signs of a disturbing immaturity. You only had to hear him attempt to muster an answer to a reporter's question to realize that the Commander in Chief was barely in command of the English language, let alone the national and international situation for which he had now once more been handed responsibility. In even the most charitable view, I could see him as no more than an affable buffoon, a lost little boy awash in the proverbial sea of troubles.

And yet . . . he had been reelected. It felt, at first, like another reminder of my powerlessness as an individual voter, a reflection of the feelings I had too frequently experienced as a writer. My voice seemed destined to resound in an endless echo chamber. Who was out there listening? So what could I do? I could sit around feeling sorry for myself and angry with my fellow Americans, but surrender and resentment seemed like poor options.

There was only one thing left for me to do: I could keep writing. It's the only thing I know how to do, and I know that I do it well. I had to say *something*. So I turned to my computer, that inestimable gift to writers. I turned it on, and, thanks to some beneficent angel—or *bodhisattava!*—who remains a mystery to me, I was guided through a series of previously unexplored byways to the Blogger. I stared at my monitor where I read an invitation to start my own blog. I had not the first idea what a blog might be, but I was certainly intrigued. Following the prompts, not knowing where they would lead me, I gave my blog a title that came to me without the benefit of thought or reflection. It was to be "The Bush Diaries." I typed it in and started my first post in the form of a tongue-in-cheek letter to the man who had just assured his return to the Oval Office.

Out of this quasi-magical moment was born what became, and remains, my daily writing practice. I did realize, after two years working on "The Bush Diaries," that I had grown weary of waking up with Bush in bed with me every morning, my head filled with thoughts about what I wanted to write to him that day; but then the blog morphed seamlessly into "The Buddha Diaries," which jogs along happily to this day. The Buddha, I promise, is a far more inspiring companion in the early hours.

The blogosphere, as I said, changed all the rules. Until that moment of discovery, my power as a writer rested eventually in the hands of others. I have always believed that writing is by definition an act of communication, and that only one half of its enactment lies in the hands of the writer. The reader is the second, indispensible element. Once written, the words call out to be published, and for this I had always been dependent on the editor of a magazine or, in the case of books, on an agent, an editor, and a publisher. To attract the initial attention, let alone the approval and collaboration of these intermediaries was, believe me, no small feat. Ask any writer. For that matter, ask any artist who has tried to find a gallery to represent her work.

Now that I had stumbled in upon the changed world of the blogosphere, I could write something every day of my life. I could publish it as I wished, without modification or approval from any meddling editor. I soon discovered I could even attract readers. I could get response. I could, in a word, communicate. I was thrilled. What more could any writer ask for?

But of course I always want more. There's the book. Even though it's now entirely possible to put out a book and market it oneself, there's always the elusive prospect of that best-seller—that gleam in the eye of every writer—which brings with it critical response, perhaps acclaim, perhaps significant financial return on all the work that went into the writing, not to mention the door that a first success will open for the next one, along with a growing readership. Who among us writers does not strive for such an opportunity?

Still, it's hard to be sanguine these days. After years of authorship—including several mid-list books put out by commercial publishers—I recognize that only the very fortunate few can expect this kind of result. So I'm grateful to be able to settle for the more intimate pleasures of the blogosphere, and especially for that small but growing coterie of readers who follow what I write; I take heart from the fact that I now have the good fortune to be a bit more than the voice crying in the wilderness. I'm able to reach people. I'm able, sometimes, to touch their lives.

I am far from the only one to have caught a glimpse of the infinite possibilities of the Internet for creative people like myself. Almost every artist I know has his or her own Web site and a network of followers, thanks to the opportunities afforded by such enterprises as Facebook and MySpace. Some have even found ways to sell their work through a proliferating number of networks that allows them to promote the things they make without that 50, sometimes 60 percent obligation to a gallery or consultant. Like many of her fellow indie musicians, my daughter has her MySpace page and posts her songs on YouTube.

All of this has come about with astonishing speed, much of it in the past ten years. Who knows, now, what the next ten years will bring? A free, open, global market place to usurp the authority of the galleries, the publishers, the producers of movies, television, and compact disks?

And what might happen to this book, I wonder, once it has been formatted, printed, made available? I trust—I know—that a few good friends will buy a copy. And some, I hope, who follow what I write in "The Buddha Diaries." Beyond that, I'd be less than honest to pretend I would not be elated if it were to find a wider readership. A lot more improbable things than this have been known to go viral thanks to the magic of the Internet. Now wouldn't that be something?

SUPERNOVA

Coinciding with my efforts to put together these thoughts about the survival of the creative spirit in a world gone mad with commerce, the shockingly premature—and apparently endlessly fascinating—death of the pop star Michael Jackson came as another blunt reminder that even mad success in the commercial world is no guarantee of genuine satisfaction or fulfillment. I have to confess that I have a poor ear for music; I never paid attention to Michael Jackson's songs and know virtually nothing about them. What I think I know about him as a pop icon and eccentric boy-man has been gleaned, over the years, from the kind of media reports that are notoriously geared to the more sensational aspects of his life than its realities. Even so, the trajectory of his creative life seems clear and sadly familiar in its outline.

The outline reads as follows: early success—amazingly early, in Jackson's case—and unsparing adulation; a childhood fraught with demands, exploitation, and outright abuse; prodigious financial returns for his work—and equally prodigious personal losses through unbridled extravagance; a troubled adult life characterized by racial and sexual ambivalence; an addiction to substance abuse and a self-destructive eating disorder to deal with the unremitting pain of having to live up to his media-created persona; paranoia brought on by the constant prying of the media and suspicion of friends and family alike . . . In sum, a cocktail guaranteed to produce a hangover of unremitting misery.

It's not a new phenomenon. Even before the Romantics came along with their tragic (pathetic?) view of the artist living at the edges of reality, bordering on madness, the reputation of the reckless, drunken, death-defying poet was long established. It's true, I think, that certain creative minds are driven to test the limits of human behavior as well as the frontiers of the human mind. Imagination is a faculty that enables the mind to run wild, to shake off the shackles of mundane reality, and to take us to places never before seen or dreamt of. Insanity is not so very different.

In any event, it seems that success, for the artist, is no easier to cope with than is failure, and even a passing acquaintance with the Buddhist teachings will remind us that both are equally illusory. The meteoric life and death of superstars in the past century alone—a constellation that would surely include the likes of Marilyn Monroe and James Dean along with the poets Dylan Thomas and Sylvia Plath and rock music idols like Janis Joplin, Jim Morrison, Jimi Hendrix, Kurt Cobain, etc.—is testimony to the unhappy truth that neither adulation nor financial reward may ever be enough. The appetite to be seen, heard, recognized, rewarded, and loved is, for some, insatiable; and the insecurities of those who experience the generous returns of a successful career are no less—and are perhaps even greater—than those who strive endlessly for those rewards without success and agonize over their supposed inadequacy.

The lesson I suppose we all must learn if we are to survive as artists, writers, musicians—creative people of all kinds—may sound like one of those cloying and irritating clichés: the only lasting, satisfying reward, if we can find it, comes from within. No amount of adulation from the world out-there will do it. No amount of material comfort, no excess of fortune is enough. We will still want more. We will still look at the work we do and judge that it's not good enough. We will still be too readily convinced that we are the transparent frauds that others will hopefully be kind enough not to see.

The hard part is to be able to experience inner satisfaction without the complacency that is, for the artist, a kind of death. The creative life is nothing if not an unending journey of the imagination, which needs the sharp edge of adventure to keep it moving forward into the unknown. Adventure implies risk; as in other walks of life, the greater the risk, the greater the reward. For Michael Jackson and those like him, more than for the rest of us, I think, the risk becomes greater with each play; and with the risk comes the danger and then, perhaps, the need for the palliative to counteract the fear. Pushed far enough for long enough, the cycle can easily end in self-destruction.

I am continually working to find a definition of success that I can live with. It's not easy, nor is it ever comfortably resolved. I watch the goalposts move, sometimes nearer, sometimes further, but always out of range unless and until I manage to get past my futile ambitions and see those goalposts for what they are: no more than a mirage, an illusion I myself create. The marvelous paradox is that I can find success in failure: I learn far more when something goes wrong with my work than when it flows along smoothly, without interruption. The tragedy of a supernova event like that of Michael Jackson is that the reverse is also true: that without that necessary sense of fulfillment that's only to be found within, even the most spectacular appearance of success is bound to taste like failure.

COMMUNITY

For my friend Kirsten, with thanks for the encouragement to get this written.

I have found a great deal of joy in community, and have three communities in particular in which I find the source of continuing—and much needed—support and love. My understanding of what community means is much influenced by what I know about the Buddhist *sangha.* I'm well aware that my reference to the term does stretch its original meaning beyond what most Buddhists would approve; one of the great traditions of that religion is known as the "Triple Gem," or the "three refuges": the Buddha himself—the enlightened one, the great teacher; the dharma, the sum of his teachings; and the *sangha*—the community.

My understanding is that the *sangha* in its original and proper sense was the religious community of monks and nuns who had made the choice to follow the path the Buddha had laid out. Here in the West, it is generally considered acceptable when used more loosely to describe even a small, informal group of people who are committed to the dharma and come together to practice meditation. The word *refuge* perfectly describes what I have personally experienced in the small sitting group of which I have been a regular member for nearly fifteen years. To go there, as I do most Sunday mornings, is to go home. It's to find a place where the noise of life abates for the time I spend there and to be in the company of people whose love for each other is simple, unquestionable, and for the most part unstated. It's just there, palpable and serene.

The group was quite tiny when I first discovered it, meeting in a secluded house on a sunny hillside. I had only recently been made aware of the rich possibilities of silent meditation. Some time before that, knowing that I was at a moment of considerable distress in my life, a friend had introduced me to Buddhism through the chanting practice of Soka Gakkai. Even though I had found the idea of meditation vaguely appealing when I had heard about it in the past, I always firmly believed that my head would never permit me to sit in silence for more than half a minute, and I seized upon chanting as a way to keep the restless part of my head occupied.

It worked, at least for a year or so, and it opened the door for everything the practice of meditation has come to mean to me since. A while later, though, I signed up for "The Core Self," a workshop with Dr. Ronald Alexander at the Esalen Institute, and was introduced slowly—a few minutes at a time at first—to the joys of silent breath meditation. What a revelation! I was soon deeply engaged. I learned that my mind could indeed be quieted, if only initially for a few brief moments. And I came rapidly to understand what the benefits of quieting the mind might be. I began to sit, almost daily, for ten minutes at first, then fifteen, then twenty.

Then I found the Laguna Sangha. Calling for information in response to an Internet lead, I was informed that the group would first sit for an hour and then take a further hour to talk about the experience of the sit as well as about aspects of the dharma. I showed up, and as usual I brought all my judgments and trepidations with me: an hour! How could I sit through a whole hour without moving, without losing my mind? And the "dharma"?

I had no idea what it was, but did it not sound suspiciously like religion, which I had long since rejected from my life?

As usually happens, though, my fears and judgments proved to be unfounded. The ideas we discussed in the after-sit session sounded like the realities of life and the experience of the mind. No God-talk—thank God! No ritual, aside from the sounding of a gong to mark the start and end of the meditation period. No one was trying to convert me.

The sit *was* hard, however. It was a struggle. My mind, predictably, was busy, no matter that I used every trick I had thus far learned to calm it down. The hour did begin to seem interminable. I began to count the minutes as they passed, each one of them seeming longer than the last. My mind kept asking, When will this ever end? My body soon grew restless too. By what must have been only halfway through the hour, my joints were screaming out in agony, desperate to be moved; there were itches everywhere, demanding to be scratched; and there was an irritation in my throat, with which I battled manfully in order not to disturb my fellow sitters.

But the hour did come to an end, and the sound of the gong brought with it a feeling of elation and relief such as I have rarely experienced. When I opened my eyes, I was overwhelmed by the serenity of the smiling faces around the circle. I have never looked back since then, and the Laguna Sangha is one of the great joys and privileges of my life. For all its silence, it is the group *par excellence*.

My second group is a community of men. There's a piece of history that needs to be inserted here. Aside from the sitting *sangha*—and indeed before I joined that group—I had already discovered the power of a small circle of people gathered together with a common purpose. Again, I'd had my share of fears and judgments to confront. Back in my younger years in the 1960s, I had heard about those "encounter groups" where men and women bared their feelings and their souls—not to mention their bodies—in pursuit of therapy, and, in keeping with my English sense of propriety, I had held such aberrant behavior in the contempt I thought it deserved. The related twelve-step programs, long proven to have helped millions in their battle with addiction, had also come in for the ungenerous ridicule that was the product of my own deeply rooted fear of revealing myself to the prying eyes of others. As I have noted previously, I had learned early in life to keep the vulnerable parts hidden from public view.

I have mentioned, too, along the way, my involvement in men's work; initially reticent in the company of other men, I had found that to sit week after week, month after month, with the small group of men that formed after an initial weekend's training gave me the opportunity to learn infinitely more about myself in listening to others—as well as the opportunity to share that who-I-am with them. It was this intense experience, along with my wife's expertise in working first-hand with artists as a coach, mentor, and advisor, which led to the formation of the third community in which I find support: our artists' groups.

Dubbed "Artists' Matters," the groups in this broad community have convened monthly at our house to share the kind of joys and challenges of the creative life that I have been discussing in these essays. The community has a good deal in common with the Laguna Sangha. We share mutual goals, common beliefs about how we want to live our lives, and common experiences. We have developed a mutual love and trust that helps us all along the path we have each chosen to follow.

The groups have shifted and changed in numbers and membership over the years, but they have proved an immensely valuable resource for all of us who participate. Most of those who join us speak of the solitude of studio, the sense of isolation in an art world that exists more as a fiction of wishful fantasy than as a reality for the vast majority of artists. We come together to find

mutual support, encouragement, and inspiration, to share the
joys as well as the disappointments, the rejections as well as the
triumphs. The only rule is that we each speak honestly and freely
and that we bring genuine concerns. We find common ground
in the sometimes-quixotic dedication we feel in the bones, and
in our pursuit of art despite all obstacles. We sit together in the
company of fellow human beings, around the metaphorical fire
we inherit from our ancient ancestors, and we know that each
one of us is loved and valued for who she or he is, and that, in
this circle, we need ask for nothing more.

These are all serious artists. I would use the word *professional*
if I believed in it, but you know I don't. When one of us succeeds
in selling a work, we all rejoice and acknowledge the achievement.
Yet not one of our number could rely on the sale of work to pay
the rent and the bills or to take care of the family. Which is why,
perhaps, we have created this other reward for ourselves—the
reward of community—where we can feel supported in the work
we do. It's a circle, one way to successfully complete the creative
circuit, whole in itself, wholly satisfying, and making whole in the
sense that it offers a very real kind of healing. It's what we need.

THE GIVEAWAY

My artist friend Gary Lloyd—the one I mentioned earlier—stopped by the other day. I have known him since the early 1970s when I walked into a gallery to see his show and was appalled by what I saw. This was before I'd had much exposure to what contemporary American artists were doing; I had learned about Picasso, Braque, and the Cubists in school. I knew a little about the Expressionists and the Surrealists, and I loved the intricate, poetic work of Paul Klee. But that was about as far as I had progressed in my acquaintance with art history. At the time, Gary was working with a variety of media, and his gallery installation included such things as axes struck into the gallery wall, strange, unidentifiable objects jerry-rigged out of cardboard, glass, and duct tape then smeared with thick coats of petroleum jelly, jars of oozing stuff that seemed to be still growing. I was confronted, brutally, with that familiar old philistine reaction: *This is art?*

I have always had one way to deal with whatever pokes an unwelcome finger into previously unexplored places of the psyche and leaves me outraged or nonplussed: I write about it. I still thought of myself primarily as a poet at that time of my life, so I went home from Gary's exhibition and wrote a twenty-five-page poem. It helped me to—I was about to say "understand," but that would not be the right word—it helped me come to terms with what I'd seen, which had sparked—along with the emotional turmoil of outright, furious rejection—a hundred different ideas and images that continued to race through my mind long afterward. I had to radically rethink my world. That was Gary's first gift. I returned it in the form of the poem I had written and was delighted when he responded to it with enthusiasm—and with a challenge: Let's make a book together.

We did. The book was called *Bob Went Home.* Its title was taken from words I'd found scrawled in childish lettering in one of the pieces in the show: "When I was a small boy, Bob went home." It struck me as a profoundly mysterious and provocative text: who was this Bob? Was he the one responsible for all this dreadful mess? Were these his broken pencils and his ink-stained book? Why did he go home? Where did he live? Were his mother and father waiting for him? Had he done something wrong and would he be punished for it? At the same time, the words led me into strangely familiar and comforting territory, as though I myself were Bob, or had been, as a small boy, and needed to get home. My poem, in a sense, was all about the Bob I had once been: clumsy and uncomfortable with my own body, forever making unintentional messes, lonely and unsure of whom I was.

Bob Went Home weighed several pounds. It had an axe handle for a spine. It had a corrugated steel cover, severely dented by the heel of a wielded axe. Its pages were made out of roofing paper, cotton pads, and thick cardboard slices slimed with Vaseline and stapled together under greaseproof paper and covered with wire mesh. The printed text—my poem—was legible only if the "reader" engaged in constant contact, constant manipulation of the physical object. It was an ungainly mammoth of a book, and Gary and I spent a good few weeks assembling multiple copies, a few of which reached the hands of collectors and the display case of at least one museum.

It had been a good long while since Gary and I had been in touch, but we'd had lunch together a couple of months before this latest visit and had vowed not to lose touch. So the other day, he came over with a gift, an artwork he had made back in 1978, "Chomsky's Boat." The piece is a construction assembled out of four large, musty tomes—directories of world writers—lined up on a rough stand made of skinned tree branches and hollowed out in the manner of a dugout canoe. If it's about anything, it's about modern communication systems and primitive ritual; about the weight and heft of things, and their fragility; about paper and books and wood; about the lasting and the ephemeral, the physicality of the material world, and the intangible, evanescent quality of the intellect and the human spirit.

It's a wonderful gift, and it gave me an entry point for this particular essay I have been ruminating on for some time now, a kind of coda to the collection. Because, in this commercial world that is so inimical to the artist and his work, the giveaway is the ultimate gesture, the spirit of generosity that I believe to be at the heart of the creative impulse.

It's not easy. The notion of professionalism—and, indeed, commercial success—is a seductive one. Most creative people I know would like nothing better than to earn a decent living doing what it is they love to do. We have been tempted, too, by the seductive promise that if we only follow our bliss, reward will surely follow. Sadly, experience teaches us otherwise. Not for all, perhaps, but for the vast majority of us, the rewards are anything but financial.

For a writer like myself, the outcome of this predicament is no worse than the hurt feelings and disappointment that go along with rejection. There is at worst a hardcopy to be filed away in some cabinet or drawer—though most of us, these days, are grateful to be able to file our stuff away on hard drives, or external drives, or in somewhere in cyberspace where they cause no inconvenience or pain. For the visual artist who accumulates years' worth of canvases or sculptural work, the problem can get to be a serious practical one of maintenance and storage.

Artworks, too, are much more tempting objects to assign value to. Lined up there, on the racks, they remind their maker of the long hours that went into their making, the cost of materials involved, the price commanded by an (obviously far inferior!) work by a friend or neighbor. Their very thing-ness seems to suggest that they must be "worth something." But what? The unpalatable truth is that the heartless law of the market applies even to artworks: they are actually worth nothing but what a ready and willing buyer will pay for them. To make matters worse, and to an absurd degree, supply inevitably exceeds demand.

The giveaway provides a surprisingly satisfying answer to this particular agony. I know from experience, because virtually everything I have written in recent years has been a giveaway. What I have written, I have posted on my blog for anyone to read, for free, at any time. In the past—and sometimes even still—I have been paid by magazines for articles; I have been paid for catalogue introductions by galleries and museums; I have even sold a few books off the shelves of Barnes & Noble, and it's nice to get the paycheck. It's very nice. It's a kind of validation that satisfies the ego even as it swells the pocketbook, even if only by a little. But I was never able to count on it, let alone make a living.

The reward for the giveaway is very different, but in some ways more satisfying still. A part of it is the freedom it allows. For me, it means I can write what I damn please, without submitting to the whims and biases of an editor. The experience of giving also comes with the pleasant feel of having committed an act of generosity with no strings attached and no expectation of return. The return, if it does come—in the form of response from a reader, praise, or even gratitude—is the proverbial icing on the cake.

But then it's easy to give something away that has no shape or substance and can be reproduced an infinite number of times without sacrifice to its integrity. It's much harder, understandably, to give away a painting or—as in Gary's case—a sculptural work that is unique and dear to the heart in the way an object can be. One artist of some note demurred when I spoke to him about the giveaway: it was, he thought, a disservice to the artist's standing in the art world, one that threatened to diminish the work itself by undercutting its value. I wondered, though, in response, what kind of value a work might have when left in the studio racks or in storage for years on end. I have been the fortunate recipient of a number of gifts over the years and value them no less for the fact that they were given. Perhaps more so, given the added value of mutual affection and recognition.

A final, scatological thought, if I may be permitted. A good part of the successful creative process consists in maintaining a flow of thought, image, and medium. A backlog of output, product, and waste can easily stop up that flow. The giveaway is one way to flush out the system, creating physical and mental space for the next effort. Give it a try; it might just work for you. But the trick is that it must be done without expectation of tangible or emotional return. It must be no less an expression of freedom than the spirit that created it. It must come, as does the work itself, purely from the heart.

MEDITATION PRACTICE

A Final Word

I keep coming back to the daily practice of meditation as the most useful of all tools in developing the persistence I need if my creative spirit and energy are to survive the challenge of these difficult times. I have already offered a couple of examples of how this practice can be done for those who might not yet be familiar with it. It feels right to conclude with one more that I find to be a useful and reliable way to get back to center, clear the mind of rubbish, and open up the flow of creativity.

Just to be clear: this is *not* what is glibly understood to be a religious or spiritual striving for transcendence—or even bliss. It's simply a pragmatic effort to train the undisciplined mind to do those things I want it to do rather than letting it run wild, reacting to whatever happens to be going on around it. Though I'll admit that bliss is an occasional and always welcome side effect.

First of all, I sit. (Perhaps it's because I came to the practice rather late in life, after my bones had already lost some of their youthful flexibility, but my body has steadfastly refused to accommodate itself to that conventional cross-legged position on the floor; I have never found it either useful or necessary to subject myself to distracting pain as strict practitioners require. I sit on a chair. But I'm aware that I get better results—as you will—if sitting upright, spine straight, forming a connection between earth and sky.) Then I close my eyes and lay the hands gently in my lap.

Breathe. That's the key. I remind myself to keep bringing the attention back to the breath. The mind will want to wander. It will want to keep itself busy, mulling over the past and worrying about the future. It's a puppy. I try to keep it on a leash, and practice pulling it gently back whenever it wants to run off and play. The breath is the leash.

In an ideal world where the activity of the brain could be easily switched off and the mind allowed to rest in pure contemplation, no guide or aid would be needed. Since we don't happen to live in an ideal world, meditation masters throughout the ages have proposed a great variety of useful crutches to help us through the process. It's one of these that I find particularly helpful.

Once focused on the breath, I take a few moments to wish myself goodwill and happiness—not the material, but the inner kind, the kind that does not impose on any other person's. Then I wish the same for my family and friends, for people I don't know and never will, people everywhere, all living beings. Wishing goodwill in this way opens up the channels of the breath even as it opens up the heart.

Next, I allow my (breathing) attention to follow a path through the body, starting with the point at the base of the torso where it's closest to the earth. I feel myself rooted, and imagine the entire body being flooded with energy flowing up from the center of the Earth—a great feeling to start out with.

From that point, I bring the attention north, to a point around the navel, where I visualize a small, golden ball radiating a special energy connected with the element of earth. I invite the mind to create the image of a landscape—rocks, mountains, deserts, rolling hills—and dwell for a moment in it; and move on to contemplate the internal, body landscape, the skeletal structure, with particular attention to the strength and stability it provides.

Next stop is the area around the solar plexus, where the same small ball is white, and the element water. I visualize water in one or many of its physical manifestations: from the smallest drop of rain to the greatest ocean. Once more, I use the breath to connect with the liquidity in the body—blood, teardrops, saliva, urine, sweat—taking note of the reality that much of its seeming solidity is in fact liquid. The human body is by some accounts up to 78 percent water. And I shift the mind into the affective experience of flow, change, and inconstancy.

Moving up to the area of the heart, I visualize the ball as red, and the element as fire. Breathing, I dwell on incandescent images, from flickering candle flames to lava flows and massive brush fires. In the body, I focus on the metabolic process by which calories are transformed into the internal heating system and the energy needed to perform the tasks of daily life. And I move, affectively, into the quality symbolized by fire: passion, experiencing that quality as it burns within the heart.

From the torso, I travel further north to the base of the throat, where each breath passes on its way into the lungs and out again when released. The ball of energy here is green, and the element is the air. To visualize the air is to see the unseeable from the traces in its wake, the movement of leaves or grasses. It's a good moment to be back in touch with the breath, taking note not only of where it enters the body, but also of the rise and fall of the shoulders, the chest, the belly. I notice, too, how air travels from the lungs into every part of the body to aerate and refresh the cells. The affective quality is inspiration. I stay with that thought for a while, and practice being "inspired."

The fifth element in the Buddhist tradition is space. You'll find its energy in the form of a blue ball at that place associated with the third eye, between and slightly above the other two. The visualization of space takes me out of body, out of this world, with a dramatic lightening effect. Inside the body, I find spaces everywhere: the orifices, yes; but I also visualize the spaces in—

and in between—the organs; and indeed, in—and in between—microscopic individual cells. I use the breath as an escort on this intricate inner journey. The affective quality of this fifth element is spaciousness. It can be felt as a physical sensation, a delicious emptiness.

You'll have noticed that we have traveled not only through the five elements, but also through the chakras. The seventh and highest chakra is at the crown of the head, where I end my meditative journey. Allowing the breath to enter through this point, I imagine it arriving from the furthest point I can imagine in the universe, bringing with it the power of absolute oneness and unquestioned knowledge. I allow myself to shed the confines of the physical body and float in the oneness that connects me to all other beings. A bit mystical perhaps. You have to experience it to understand . . .

And last, I allow the breath to flow through me, from that furthest point of the universe to the center of the earth and back in the opposite direction, with my body acting as no more than the medium through which energy travels. It's here that you might have the experience of bliss, along with the freeing of all those channels you need to open up in order to get back to work with renewed energy and renewed inspiration. Believe me, it works. And it's well worth the ride.

ABOUT PETER CLOTHIER

Peter Clothier's prior publications include two novels, two books of poetry and a monograph on the British artist David Hockney, along with scores of articles and reviews on art and books in national journals. His memoir, "While I Am Not Afraid: Secrets of a Man's Heart", has been widely praised as the authentic story of one man's path to personal integrity.

Having served as an educator and an art school dean variously at the University of Southern California, Otis Art Institute and Loyola Marymount University, Clothier left academia many years ago to devote himself full time to his writing. He still describes himself as a "recovering academic." A student of the dharma who follows a daily meditation practice, he is the author of the online weblog, "The Buddha Diaries"; his political passions find their outlet in his regular contributions to The Huffington Post. To find out more about Clothier's life and work, visit his Web site at PeterClothier.com.